IN THE
DARK BEFORE
DAWN

OTHER THOMAS MERTON BOOKS
PUBLISHED BY
NEW DIRECTIONS

IN THE DARK BEFORE DAWN

NEW SELECTED POEMS OF

THOMAS MERTON

EDITED WITH AN INTRODUCTION
AND NOTES BY
LYNN R. SZABO

PREFACE BY
KATHLEEN NORRIS

A NEW DIRECTIONS BOOK

Book design by Sylvia Frezzolini Severance
Manufactured in the United States of America
New Directions Books are published on acid-free paper.
First published as New Directions Paperbook 1005 in 2005
Published simultaneously in Canada by Penguin Books Canada Limited

Library of Congress Cataloging in Publication Data

Merton, Thomas, 1915–1968
    In the dark before dawn : new selected poems of Thomas Merton /
edited with an introduction and notes by Lynn R. Szabo:
preface by Kathleen Norris.
        p. cm.
Includes bibliographical references and index.
    ISBN 978-0-8112-1613-5 (alk. paper)
I. Szabo, Lynn. II. Title.
    PS3525.E7174A6 2005
    811'.54—dc22
                                        2004030957
Fourth Printing

New Directions Book are published for James Laughlin
by New Directions Publishing Corporation,
80 Eighth Avenue, New York, NY 10011

I think poetry must
I think poetry must
Stay open all night
In beautiful cellars

Canto 53
—from *Cables to the Ace* (1968)

TABLE OF CONTENTS

The prolific writer Thomas Merton had much to say to the world, but his poems are the fruit of listening. Merton recognized early on that in an increasingly violent and cacophonous world, the ability to listen is constrained, and even threatened. Particularly in his verse, he became a prophet of language. In *Cables to the Ace*, Merton speaks of "Words replaced by moods. Actions punctuated by the hard fall of imperatives. More and more smoke . . . No one need attend. Listening is obsolete. So is silence." (150) Writing in the late 1960s, Merton foresaw the relentless onslaught of commercial and political verbiage that so distracts and wearies us in the early twenty-first century.

"Listen" is the first word of St. Benedict's Rule for monks, and in order to hear well, one must be quiet. If today both silence and listening are difficult to find, increasingly relegated to the realm of the monastery, it is also true that those monasteries are much in demand. The guest quarters at Merton's abbey of Gethsemani, like those of many Benedictine and Trappist monasteries in America, are often booked a year in advance. It would appear that monks, the inheritors of a 1,700-year-old Christian tradition, and the silence they foster, are not anachronistic, but more necessary than ever.

All poets must learn to listen, in the words of Benedict, "with the ear of the heart." (RB Prologue; 1) They must learn to nurture a certain quality of attention that lends itself to the writing of verse. The poet who is a monk lives in a way that intensifies this process, as a life pared down to its essentials encourages close attention to the resonant tones of scripture and the lighter notes of wind and birdsong. Monks spend a good part of their time listening to one another recite scripture and the poetry of the psalms, and their days remain stubbornly in tune with the rural rhythms of sunrise and sunset. It is appropriate, as Merton's former teacher, the poet Mark Van Doren, once noted, that "sound is somehow for Merton the carrying sense, the medium through which experience of any magnitude makes itself seen and felt." (Merton's *Selected Poems*, 1967 ed., xv)

In this book we hear moonlight ringing "upon the ice as sudden as a footstep" (53) and the cries of playing children, "Clear as water," their words coming from a distance, "words that flower / On little voices, light as stems of lilies." (77) We stand with Merton in the cemetery at Gethsemani and hear "the treble harps of night begin to play in the deep wood..." praising the "holy sleep" of the monks buried there, as "all the frogs along the creek / Chant in the moony waters to the Queen of Peace." (33)

A vast hospitality is contained in these spare lines, as trees, insects, frogs, the moon, the Blessed Virgin, and the remembered dead are each acknowledged and made welcome. The generous gesture is typical of Merton and echoes an earlier poem, "For My Brother: Reported Missing in Action, 1943," in which he summons for his brother Christ's tears that fall silently, "Like bells upon your alien tomb. / Hear them and come: they call you home." (181) To venture a dangerously worn word, Merton has a mystic's sense of unity, and in his poems he wants to bring as much together as he can. Sometimes he does it with monastic simplicity, as in the brief, poignant "Song for Nobody," in which a sunflower is seen as a "gentle sun" in whose "dark eye / somebody is awake," and heard as it "Sings without a word / By itself." (95)

But Merton can also insist on plenitude, and a wild extravagance flowers in much of his work, such as a lengthy meditation of flying out of O'Hare during the 1960s. He asks, "Should the dance of Shivashapes / All over flooded prairies / Make hosts of (soon) Christ-Wheat / Self-bread which could also be / Squares of Buddha-Rice . . . " (167) The farmland and rivers he passes over flood him with images of Vietnamese villages in flames, generals giving news conferences, and the literature of his boyhood, the adventures of both Tom Swift and Huckleberry Finn. Flying west, over South Dakota, he envisions Mount Rushmore as "four Walt Whitmans / Who once entrusted the nation to rafts," and hears a politician lying, promising a weapon, presumably napalm, that as "a mildly toxic invention can harm none / But the enemy." (170)

The thematic organization of this book allows the reader to journey with Merton through the themes that were most important to him: being in many different landscapes and staying in one place, worshiping and contemplating, being a person of faith in a world of doubt and fully engaging with that world. Merton repays the world with constant, close attention, amplified by wit, humor, and a no-nonsense, finely tuned bullshit detector. He writes with both praise and scorn of cities, recognizing that they are full of human beings, and thus opportunities for grace: "Here in the jungles of our waterpipes and iron ladders, / Our thoughts are quieter than rivers, / Our loves are simpler than the trees, / Our prayers deeper than the sea." (25) But the city also is fueled by cruel economies that allow an American executive to swim in India, in "chlorinated / Indigo water where no / Slate-blue buffalo has ever / Got wet," (21) while ignoring the impoverished children playing in dust hard by the hotel's front door.

What may be most valuable for the contemporary reader is the way that Merton's poems offer evidence that ecstasy, and specifically religious ecstasy, is still possible in this world, and still meaningful. In a poem that evokes George Herbert, Merton writes, "When psalms surprise me with their music / And antiphons turn to rum / The Spirit sings: the bottom drops out of my soul." In the daily ritual of psalmody, which can become tedious for a monk, Merton unexpectedly finds love within himself, thundering forth "from the center of my cellar," until "songs grow up around me like a jungle." He is in Eden, with animals joining the chorus. "I am drunk," he writes, "with the great wilderness / Of the sixth day in Genesis." Of course he fails to sustain the mood, and ordinary fears resurface, along with the demands of the day. "And I go forth with no more wine and no more stars / And no buds and no more Eden / And no more animals and no more sea." He takes some comfort in knowing that Eden does exist, and God still sings there "by Himself in acres of night / And walls fall down, that guarded Paradise." (83–84)

Of a lesser garden and gardener, Merton writes, in the touching "Elegy for a Trappist," of a confrere, a "Master of the sudden enthusiastic gift," who would hide home-grown bouquets in his cowl and place them in church. Astonishingly, it is a delivery truck that provides Merton with the perfect elegiac metaphor. Its headlights illuminate, briefly, the deceased monk's abandoned garden, which returns to darkness as the gates close, and Merton observes that it is "As if Leviathan / Hot on the scent of some other blood / Had passed you by / And never saw you hiding in the flowers." (43–44) This is a love poem of the first order, one of many in this book.

It is said of Abba Anthony, one of the first and most renowned Christian monks, that pilgrims to the desert knew him at once, even in a gathering of brothers, by the glow of hospitality he exuded. I think of these poems in that way, as welcoming all comers. It does not require a believer to comprehend Merton's sense of Christ, as a presence in his life, even before he became a monk: "You were my France and England, / My seas and my America . . . / Oh, when I loved You, even while I hated You, / Loving and yet refusing You in all the glories of your universe." (54–55) It does not require a Christian to identify with either Merton's desire for God or the doubt that follows on its heels: "Christ rises on the cornfields / It is only the harvest moon." (156)

Anyone who has ever awakened in a hospital bed can readily identify with the disorientation Merton feels as illness leads him to "wonder who the hell I am." (188) The sounds of hospital machinery become freight trains and airliners flying on the jet stream, mocking him, as Christ was mocked. "I am Christ's lost cell / His childhood and desert age / His descent into hell." If

Christ is also love, that love remains "without need and without name . . . the spark without identity..." (190) The question of identity was always a loaded one for Merton. Was he French? American? A Christian monk vowed to stability? A wanderer of the world and explorer of its various religions? Was he a celibate? A lover? Like Walt Whitman, Thomas Merton contained multitudes: he was all of these, and more.

In a prose poem, the meditative "Hagia Sophia," Merton writes of being awakened in a hospital bed by a nurse's voice, and in a Whitmanesque turn, finding, "I am like all mankind awakening from all the dreams that ever were dreamed in all the nights of the world." (65) It is a feast of the Virgin, of Wisdom, Merton notes, and his religious imagination takes fire. "It is like being awakened by Eve. It is like being awakened by the Blessed Virgin. It is like coming forth from primordial nothingness and standing in clarity, in Paradise." (66) Merton's previous collections of verse have included poems referring, in more or less veiled terms, to this hospital experience, and the nurse he befriended there. In this volume the love poems he wrote about their relationship appear in all their honest emotion. They are giddy, even adolescent, as the adult Merton is humbled by the experience of love and overwhelmed by being in love with love. At times the poems are flippant—Merton thinks of his absent lover "In my solitary swamp amid the hot frog blues" (208)—but they are also profoundly religious: "Because I am always broken / I obey my nurse / Who in her grey eyes and her mortal breast / Holds an immortal love the wise have fractured / Because we have both been broken we can tell / That God did not make death." (194)

Late in his life, Merton was apparently blessed to discover that a loving relationship creates the "whole world / Over again," until "There is only this one love / Which is now our world . . . / Celebrated by all the poets / Since the first beginning / Of any song." (197) He and the woman are Adam and Eve, and as Christ is both present and absent to Merton the monk, his beloved is absent, and yet present to Merton the man: "You wake in me, darling / We are nearer than we know / Love has another / Place of its own / Nearer to you than hill or city / Nearer than your own mirror . . . " (219) The honesty of this verse is compelling, as Merton wishes, hard, "If you and I could even start again as strangers," and laments, "If only you and I / were possible." (218) The reader can be grateful that these words were possible, and necessary, for Merton to write. If these poems reflect his way of listening to the world, with all of its glory and pain, they also require that we listen in return, and as well.

KATHLEEN NORRIS

INTRODUCTION

When Thomas Merton was awarded the literary prize for the author of the "best example of English verse" at Columbia University in 1939, he was announced as one of the poets of the young generation who was "aware of the living present and all it may hold of pain and purpose." In the nearly seven decades since, Merton's eleven volumes and numerous extant manuscripts of poetry have demonstrated the foresight of that claim. He has now secured his stature in the pantheon of important twentieth-century American poets.

His iconoclasm, always in tension with his contemplative and writerly temperaments, readily places him in conversation with the past voices of solitaries such as H.D. Thoreau and Emily Dickinson, but also in tandem with the profound influences of contemporaries whom he appropriated as literary mentors: James Joyce, T.S. Eliot, W.H. Auden, Robert Lowell, William Carlos Williams, Denise Levertov, and some of the Beats. Merton claimed that the most profound aesthetic influence on his poetry was the highly esteemed German poet Rainer Maria Rilke. His spiritual quest led him into a lifelong study of the luminous religious poets William Blake and Gerard Manley Hopkins. He was enchanted by the Persian poet Rumi and absorbed by the holy writings of Buddhism and Hinduism. The subversive, political ethos of the twentieth-century Spanish and Latin-American poets, Federico García Lorca, Nicanor Parra, Pablo Neruda, Pablo Antonio Cuadra, and Miguel Grinberg was the inspiration for Merton's antipoetry of the late 1960s. Merton's profound letters engaged the literary friendships of Nobel Prize–winners Boris Pasternak and later, Czeslaw Milosz, who became a devoted correspondent and colleague (their letters have been collected in the fascinating volume, *Striving Towards Being,* 1996, edited by Robert Faggen). Merton's genius nearly overwhelms the reader, when one considers that the formation of his poetics derived in most part from his reading and correspondence, even though he received, particularly in the later years at Gethsemani, a plethora of literary, political, cultural, and religious figures who came to engage him in personal dialogue.

Since Merton began his career as a published poet, his poetry has never been out of print; it is now becoming a focus not only for scholars and readers in the tradition of English literature but is also increasingly appearing in new foreign translations. Fugitive poems are continuously being discovered, providing both juvenilia and posthumous evidence of Merton's lifelong poetic inclinations. Even in his earliest extant poems (written when he was a schoolboy in England), we are notified of the various poses and issues his voice would embrace in the subsequent decades when he wrote thousands of poems: questions about historical events, philosophy, contemporary literature, culture and anthropology, religion, and language. In "Ermine Street," printed in his school newspaper, *The Oakhamian,* just before Merton's sixteenth birthday (and brought to light in 1998), one sees the intimations of his uncanny ability to telescope the events of the past, present, and future into a single landscape:

On Sussex strand there beached the Roman keel;
On Sussex downs there flashed the Roman steel:
'Till westwards Britons fled from Sussex Shore,
And Ermine street was built with spoils of war.

. . . Yet now both hoof and horn have died away,
And there has dawned a less romantic day.
The Glasgow 'bus seeks Scotland's fog bound shore,
And Stamford trembles at its thund'ring roar.

1931

Just below these stanzas appeared a six-line French verse by the young Merton—a precursor of his aptitude for writing poetry in other languages which would demonstrate itself throughout his life, as did his fancy for translating it from them.

One of the compelling attractions for those who read his writings is his relentless pursuit of authenticity both in his journey to self-knowledge and his understanding of the social order. The cultural critique allowed by Merton's choice of vocation as a self-marginalizing monk of the Abbey of Gethsemani also appeals to many readers who seek relief from the technological displacement of current Western culture. His profound dialogue with the East and its religious and cultural traditions culminated in his conferences with His Holiness the Dalai Lama while on a rarely permitted monastic pilgrimage in Asia in 1968. Merton's study of Zen wisdom draws readers into worldviews that explore vistas of contemplation and meditation outside of Western traditions. His nearly encyclopedic aggregation of multidisciplinary reading and thought informs his readers of the uniquely integrative patterns in his poetics. Yet Merton the charismatic man is never far from Merton the iconoclastic poet, lending readers access to both at once, while at the same time engendering an amplitude of possibilities for engagement and interpretation.

Thomas Merton's single most important gift to his readers was his prophetic vocation to perceive and distinguish in his art the fundamental unity in the cosmos. His understanding of the "hidden Wholeness" of all things is embedded in his apprehension of the transcendent in the immanent. Those who read Thomas Merton's work are magnetized by his unyielding search for meaning and significance in the face of the ironies of disintegration and fragmentation currently associated with postmodern perspectives on art and language. Merton's approach to his quest for meaning and unity as it unfolds in his now many published volumes of journals, spiritual writings, and lively correspondence resonates with the hopes and desires of the citizens of the new millennium.

Merton's place as a marginal person arising from his monastic vows and the silence elected by the Trappist monks offers his readers poetry in which the geography of space and time for reflection and imagination is held sacred. His seeming transparency makes accessible his sacred pathway to self-knowledge acquired throughout the more than five decades before and during his monastic life at the Abbey of Gethsemani near Louisville, Kentucky. The silence Merton so loved and sought creates an ethos in his poetry which serves as the bas-relief for the sculpting of sound as an expression of silence, rather than its interruption.

Merton's origins had forerun his capabilities as an artist and contemplative. His parents, Ruth Jenkins and Owen Merton, met in Paris when both went there to study art. Ruth was an American born in the Midwest, whose father had moved the family to Long Island Sound in order for him to pursue a career in publishing. Ruth and Owen Merton, a New Zealander who was a talented musician as well as an artist, were married during the Easter holiday in England in 1914.

At the outbreak of World War I, the young couple relocated to Prades, in the Catalan region of France. They intended to continue their lives as artists there in the Languedoc, which had nourished so many others of their kind. There, on January 31, 1915, Tom Merton was born, as he writes in the powerful words that begin his now classic autobiography, *The Seven Storey Mountain* (1949), "free by nature, in the image of God . . . ." In those sunny regions where his first encounters with the natural world and the language of human discourse occurred, his prescient ear and eye found the source which created the music and imagery of his many lyric poems. Not until later did Merton begin to discover that he was also "the prisoner of [his] own violence and [his] own selfishness . . . the image of the world into which [he] was born."

But the young family's idyllic encounter with paradise was short-lived when, in 1915, they relocated to America, far away from the dangers of the spreading European conflagrations. There

Merton's brother, John Paul, was born in 1918 and there Ruth Merton succumbed to stomach cancer when Merton was just six years old. Her loss would retain its unimaginable impact throughout his life, particularly recorded in his many dreamscapes where the feminine presents itself in the form of a dark-eyed Jewish girl named Proverb, as *Hagia Sophia*—the feminine wisdom of God— and as a nurse with special healing powers. (His later devotion to the Virgin Mary has been analyzed by Jungian and Freudian psychoanalysts as an expression of his strong desire to know the feminine in the depths of his psyche.)

Owen Merton subsequently took the six-year-old Tom with him on itinerant travels and short-lived domestic arrangements in the Caribbean and Bermuda. This talented young father was acquiring his strengths as a watercolorist and landscape painter but his inadequacies as a parent led to an unstable and lonely life for a young school-age child. Eventually, father and son settled in France where Owen intended to paint in and around the medieval village of St. Antonin in the Noble Valley.

A child full of wonder and intensity, Tom Merton began to absorb the experiences which would mark his poetic consciousness for the next half century. His schooldays were almost entirely miserable but he demonstrated his acuity with awards in everything from sports to languages. He attended the local Lycée and then was sent to Oakham School for boys in England in 1929. In the worst of fortunes, Owen Merton died of brain cancer when Tom was a student at Oakham, leaving him an orphan at fifteen. In 1932, he sat for the entrance examination to Cambridge, was awarded a place as a reader in the classics and in 1935, he returned to America after a series of academic and social disasters. He enrolled at Columbia University where he became a man about campus, cartoonist, editor, and sportsman, with considerable success. His avocation for writing flourished along with the lively friendships of other aspiring writers and artists, including Robert Lax, Ad Reinhardt, and Ed Rice.

Merton had expressed his talent for writing throughout his childhood and youth. He had kept a journal since at least the age of sixteen and had written a number of stories and even a short novel in his early teens. His mother reports in her records of his infant life, "Tom's Book," that he could read, write, and draw by the age of five. At the age when most North American students are beginning their attempts at literacy, Tom was beginning to read the classics in Latin, French, and German. When he finished his undergraduate degree at Columbia, he had already submitted a novel to a number of New York publishers and was writing reviews for *The New York Times*. He wanted to be a renowned writer.

Merton's early life mirrored the privileges of wealth tainted by what he called his "poverty of spirit," and by the time he was a graduate student, he had exhausted himself in the pursuit of meaningful experience and social influence. He had dabbled in various political movements and volunteered at Catherine de Hueck's Friendship House in Harlem. Unaware of it, Merton was poised for a profound religious conversion. In 1938, while he was reading G.F. Lahey's life of G.M. Hopkins and Étienne Gilson's *The Spirit of Medieval Philosophy*, the frustrated intellectual and repressed spiritual longings of his circumstances moved him to seek to become a Catholic. In a remarkable story of its own, recorded in *The Seven Storey Mountain*, Merton recounts how by December of 1941 he had made the radical choice to become a Trappist monk of the Abbey of Gethsemani near Louisville, Kentucky. He would join the Cistercian Order of the Strictest Observance (the official name of the Trappists) and eventually take the solemn vows of poverty, obedience, and stability—the commitment to remain with his chosen order until his death, which he did until his life ended tragically in 1968, when he died of electrocution on his Asian journey.

The best of Merton's poetry, like that of other successful poets, mediates his artistic vision and its representation through metaphor that is powerful and direct in its influences. But Merton's unique poetics are grounded in and influenced by two fundamental and ironic singularities: his refusal to dichotomize the secular and the sacred and his vocation to the contemplative life of the Cistercian monastic. His identity became grounded in his vocation, engendering the language by which to represent his experience beyond the realm of empiricism and metaphysics and birthing a sophisticated and penetrating wisdom arising from the analogous worlds of the poet and the mystic.

At its finest, Merton's poetry depicts itself in the language of symbology that represents the ontological and psychological parallels of these worlds. He explained in his book *Love and Living* that "the true symbol does not merely point to some hidden object. It contains in itself a structure which . . . makes us aware of the inner meaning of life and reality itself. . . . A true symbol takes us to the center not to another point on the circumference."

Integrated into the canon of his poetry are the wide-ranging subjects of his literary and personal experience and, more importantly, social and religious commentary of perspicacious and prophetic insight. His genius was to create an artistic vision fuelled by the conflict between his calling as a writer and his vocation as a contemplative. It is this conflict that grounds the discourse, rhetoric, syntactical strategies, and metaphorical language for most of his vast poetic corpus. His anxiety about the existential dilemma created by the debasement of language in modern American culture led him through and away from conventional paradigms for poetry and ultimately towards an antipoetry that sought to engage and rout the powerful tensions which erupt when the limitations of language distort and disrupt its possibility for meaning.

Impressive renderings of Merton's singular artistic vision resonate throughout his poetry and are limited neither to their forms nor to an evolving chronological progression. From his earliest interests in writing poetry, Merton's voice demonstrates its capacity for reflection and synthesis, focusing on vast and broad-ranging complexities in the human story and on experiences far beyond his own. In the pattern of a Dantesque spiral of epiphanies, he continuously navigates the geography of his inner and exterior worlds, with new and maturing perspectives. In the rewarding study of his large body of poetry, one observes his repeated engagement with the same vexed questions throughout.

What is most compelling about his poetic voice is the magnetism and charisma of its temperament and resonances. He continued, throughout his monastic life, to explore and develop poetry that wove together the synthesis of both worlds (monastic and secular) of which he remained a deeply insightful and committed citizen. Poems that Merton was writing as a young student and monk appeared in prestigious journals and magazines, including *The New Yorker* and *Poetry*. That his earlier poems often center on life at the Abbey of Gethsemani is not as important as their representation of his determination to synthesize his newfound spiritual life with the enormous range of experience he had already accumulated as a young man in his mid-twenties. Although the voicing of these poems sometimes lacks the literary skill and sophistication Merton unpacks in his later poetry, the intensity of his insight and his deep concern about human society is equally as apparent.

The most significant figure in his early literary career was Professor Mark Van Doren, eminent man of letters at Columbia University and Merton's lifelong mentor and friend. It was to Professor Van Doren that Merton gave nearly all of his writings just before leaving for the Abbey of Gethsemani on December 10, 1941. The collection of their letters and Merton's manuscripts at the Rare Book Room of the Columbia University library is one of the most important extant records of Merton's literary life. It was Van Doren who first recommended Merton to James Laughlin of New Directions and made the selection of poems for Merton's first published volume, *Thirty Poems,* in 1944. Laughlin became the publisher of nearly all of the volumes of Merton's poetry.

Van Doren remained Merton's critic, confidant, and champion, offering his wisdom and fatherly love to the young monk whose quest it was to exist in the tension between his art and his vocation.

Merton's early prescience about the linguistic turn in literary and cultural theory retained its integrity throughout his writing life. He was prophetic in diagnosing the origins of irony and cynicism about language and its potentially defeating limitations. When he read Roland Barthes' *Writing Degree Zero* (1950), he quickly responded with an incisive essay, "Writing as Temperature," which demonstrated his insight into the conceptual framework that foregrounded postmodern literary theory. Barthes had put words to the poetics Merton had been engaging since the late 1930s, when he wrote his satirical critique in the poem "The Philosophers" and the motif of what would later become his morality play in verse, *The Tower of Babel*. In the mid-'60s, he would publish his antipoetry, *Cables to the Ace*, in which the entire collection of cantos is predicated on the debasement of language that erupts when form and meaning are fractured by its users:

> Since language has become a medium in which we are immersed, there is no longer any need to say anything. The saying says itself all around us. No one need attend. Listening is obsolete . . . . (Some of the better informed have declared war on language). (Canto 3)

Merton's response to this dilemma was to engage metaphor and its tropes as the medium by which language can be set free from its limitations; thus, it becomes the agency for the expression of the human imagination, offering limitless possibilities for creation and incarnation. In a 1938 review of John Crowe Ransom's *The World's Body,* Merton had written that poetry is a "kind of knowledge . . . that cannot be gained by any other means, for the poet is concerned with the aspects of experience that can never be well-described, but only reproduced or imitated." For him, metaphor, the medium of all poetry, represented an infinite desire to acknowledge invisible and unknown realities, the attempt to express the inexpressible and transcend the confines of language itself. In the poetry selected for this volume, metaphor proves itself in its confrontation with the seemingly dichotomous, going beyond both metaphysics and empiricism. With wit and humor, Merton portrays his refusal to be defeated by the notion that *logos* has been irreparably fractured, form from meaning. He wrote three seminal essays in which he manifests his poetics in the face of modernist controversies, literary, religious, and political: "Message to Poets," "Poetry and Contemplation: A Reappraisal," and "Poetry, Symbolism, and Typology."

Merton came to embrace the profound relationship that developed between his vocation to the silence of his monastic life and its rich and sacralizing effects on his poetics. Against all expectation and in spite of the persistent efforts of the Catholic Church to silence him in the '60s, Merton emerged as one of the most prominent and effective social critics in twentieth-century America. This irony is not lost on the profound conflict Merton experienced between a vocation to monastic solitude and the expression of his relentless social conscience. Words were his enemies as much as they were his allies, circumscribing him with guilt as often as they articulated his longing for freedom for humanity.

But ultimately, silence and solitude create the conditions of a "beautiful terror" that is the paradoxical force at the center of Merton's poetics. From them emanate the hiddenness, complexity, and mystery that are the categories for many of his poems. Silence becomes the fertile ground of his prolific writings, and at the heart of his vexation about the seeming contradictions of the contemplative and writerly lives there is an inner core of transcendent values—silence, peace, and transformational experience—that fuels the centrifugal force at the center of his poetics. Those values impelled his perpetual search for authenticity, leading him away from the devoutly religious, and toward the social and political: American civil rights and the Vietnam War, for example. At the deepest level, Merton experienced the mystic's profound understanding that silence is a language of its own with as much influence and power as words (his study and practice of Zen was of great importance to this revelation). His poetics "dances in the water of life," in which sound and silence create their own music and art.

Thomas Merton remained all his life a marginal man observing and reconfiguring for his readers what it means to be authentic in a secular society. As he embraced his search, he courageously and prophetically spoke out against all threats to peace and safety for his American compatriots, while at the same time he persistantly sought unity with all humanity.

When the first *Selected Poems* appeared in America in 1959, Mark Van Doren introduced it by acclaiming Merton's poetry, even though Merton himself wrote in the letter of request for the introduction that he believed that "a poet's only book is his collected poems" and that when his were collected, "a lot [would] have to go." That edition was enlarged in 1967. The current selection seeks to include more poems from the latter period of Merton's writings, with considerable representation of the antipoetry collected in *Cables to the Ace* (1967) and *The Geography of Lograire* (1968). The poems appear as they do in *The Collected Poems of Thomas Merton*—except for evident errors, the inclusion of new material, and design features. Otherwise, they have been taken from books and manuscripts elsewhere available (see Notes, pp. 237–46).

A number of foreign editions of his poetry, some in translation, have appeared, as well. In 1950, based on the three volumes of his poems that had been published by then, a British edition was selected and introduced by Robert Speaight, in which he explained that Merton's labor had been "to refine his experience into aesthetic form." His praise of Merton's poetic skills was somewhat muted, based on such early evidence, but it is now apparent that his enthusiasm can be endorsed and elaborated. The appearance of Merton's poems in a number of anthologies of American verse during the course of his life and since is indicative of this.

In making the selections for this volume, I have responded to a number of criteria by which the reader might have access to a robust and aesthetic appreciation of Merton's poems. In studying the canon of Merton's poetry, one observes that his work engages themes which continue to reappear throughout. In this way, he approaches a stable of issues that informs his worldview and artistic vision from his youth to his death. It seemed worthwhile then to arrange the selection thematically. One advantage would be to allow readers to follow his aesthetic and spiritual responses to these issues as his social and artistic consciousness matured and developed into that of a noteworthy American poet. At the same time, this thematic arrangement allows readers to observe quite readily shifts in his poetics as he represents these themes in his poetry. In providing dates for their publication in volume collections, I have wanted to assist readers somewhat with their chronology. The careful dating of composition is a study still ahead for scholars who must perhaps await more specific and accurate manuscript evidence. (Note: although not published separately until 1971, I have indicated the composition dates for *Early Poems*.)

The selections for this edition arose from their literary quality, which I defined by their value in representing the integrity of Merton's aesthetic vision as a writer and a monk, carefully studied in relation to his other writings collected in his notebooks, journals, and essays. Moreover, the many variegations in his compelling personality and his private world are represented in this selection, including the poems of love written to a young nurse he met while in hospital and to whom he formed a special attachment when he was in his early fifties. (These poems, up until now, have been available only in *Eighteen Poems,* a special edition of two hundred and fifty copies produced by James Laughlin in 1985 and held, for the most part, in private collections.)

The title for this selection, *In the Dark Before Dawn: New Selected Poems of Thomas Merton,* reflects Merton's love of the predawn hours, after the Night Vigils monastic office, in which he found the silent darkness to be the ground of his creative energies, fed by contemplation and the rising sun. The phrase is taken from his lovely "Elegy for a Trappist," a lament that captured the prophetic voice embedded in Merton's self-transcendence and poetics. The eight sections to which I've assigned the selections of this volume represent seminal aspects of Merton's engagement of his inner and outer worlds throughout his life. Their themes are emblematic of his life and his art, synthesizing the apparent dichotomies of his monasticism and his poetry: silence and language, anonymity and renown, asceticism and art, mysticism and secularism, contemplation and action. It is in these paradoxes that Merton's poetry sounds its songs of integrity, wisdom, and hope in the face of the confounding history of twentieth-century America and invites his readers into his portraiture of that "beautiful terror" which is the human condition. The endnotes are provided to enable the reader to establish unknown contexts and avoid obvious misinterpretations. Although in its early stages, significant and valuable scholarship on Merton's poetry readily awaits the reader who is drawn to the rewarding research of his corpus.

To the many allies who have made this edition possible, I am profoundly grateful: first, to Peggy Fox and Peter Glassgold of New Directions, who have been at the helm throughout; equally, to the Trustees of the Merton Legacy Trust (especially Anne McCormick), for their support and permission to reproduce the poems in this volume. Many friends in Merton scholarship have offered insight and direction as I have worked my way through the poetry to this selection: Ross Labrie, Canada's foremost Merton scholar, whose wisdom has mentored me for more than a decade; George Kilcourse of Bellarmine University; the Archivists of the Merton Studies Center there, Jonathan Montaldo and Paul Pearson; Michael Higgins of St. Jerome's University; Patrick O'Connell, the meticulous editor of *The Merton Seasonal*, whose remarkable collegiality and support have lent helpful insight to this process; Michael Mott, whose excellent biography of Merton,

The Seven Mountains of Thomas Merton, has provided the context in which to view the entirety of Merton's poetry and prose; Br. Paul Quenon, poet and student of Thomas Merton at the Abbey of Gethsemani, whose fine translations of the French poems are included here; Br. Patrick Hart, Merton's secretary and posthumous editor, who has shown friendship and interest in my work on Merton's behalf; and Patrick Lawlor and his colleagues in the Rare Book Room at the Columbia University library. My research and writing has been greatly assisted by the Social Sciences and Humanities Research Council of Canada, by my designation as a Shannon Fellow of the International Thomas Merton Society, and by my very competent assistant, Alexandra Moore.

LYNN R. SZABO

ONE

GEOGRAPHY'S LANDSCAPES

THE NIGHT TRAIN

In the unreason of a rainy midnight
France blooms along the windows
Of my sleepy bathysphere,
And runs to seed in a luxuriance of curious lights.

Escape is drawn straight through my dream
And shines to Paris, clean as a violin string,
While spring tides of commotion,
(The third-class pianos of the Orient Express)
Fill up the hollow barrels of my ears.

Cities that stood, by day, as gay as lancers
Are lost, in the night, like old men dying.
At a point where polished rails branch off forever
The steels lament, like crazy ladies.
We wake, and weep the deaths of the cathedrals
That we have never seen,
Because we hear the jugulars of the country
Fly in the wind, and vanish with a cry.

At once the diplomats start up, as white as bread,
Buckle the careless cases of their minds
That just fell open in the sleeper:

For, by the rockets of imaginary sieges
They see to read big, terrible print,
Each in the other's face,

That spells the undecoded names
Of the assassins they will recognise too late:
The ones that seem to be secret police,
Now all in place, all armed, in the obvious ambush.   *1944*

AUBADE: LAKE ERIE

When sun, light handed, sows this Indian water
With a crop of cockles,
The vines arrange their tender shadows
In the sweet leafage of an artificial France.

Awake, in the frames of windows, innocent children,
Loving the blue, sprayed leaves of childish life,
Applaud the bearded corn, the bleeding grape,
And cry:
"Here is the hay-colored sun, our marvelous cousin,
Walking in the barley,
Turning the harrowed earth to growing bread,
And splicing the sweet, wounded vine.
Lift up your hitch-hiking heads
And no more fear the fever,
You fugitives, and sleepers in the fields,
Here is the hay-colored sun!"

And when their shining voices, clean as summer,
Play, like churchbells over the field,
A hundred dusty Luthers rise from the dead, unheeding,
Search the horizon for the gap-toothed grin of factories,
And grope, in the green wheat,
Toward the wood winds of the western freight.   *1944*

THE OHIO RIVER—LOUISVILLE

No one can hear the loud voice of the city
Because of the tremendous silence
Of this slow-moving river, quiet as space.

Not the towering bridge, the crawling train,
Not the knives of pylons
Clashing in the sun,
And not the sky-swung cables;
Not the outboard boat
Swearing in the fiery distance like a locust,
Not the iron cries of men:
Nothing is heard,
Only the immense and silent movement of the river.

The trains go through the summer quiet as paper,
And, in the powerhouse, the singing dynamos
Make no more noise than cotton.
All life is quieter than the weeds
On which lies lightly sprawling,
Like white birds shot to death,
The bathers' clothing.

But only where the swimmers float like alligators,
And with their eyes as dark as creosote
Scrutinize the murderous heat,
Only there is anything heard:
The thin, salt voice of violence,
That whines, like a mosquito, in their simmering blood.   *1946*

AUBADE—HARLEM

for Baroness C. de Hueck

Across the cages of the keyless aviaries,
The lines and wires, the gallows of the broken kites,
Crucify, against the fearful light,
The ragged dresses of the little children.
Soon, in the sterile jungles of the waterpipes and ladders,

The bleeding sun, a bird of prey, will terrify the poor,
These will forget the unbelievable moon.

But in the cells of whiter buildings,
Where the glass dawn is brighter than the knives of surgeons,
Paler than alcohol or ether, shinier than money,
The white men's wives, like Pilate's,
Cry in the peril of their frozen dreams:

"Daylight has driven iron spikes,
Into the flesh of Jesus' hands and feet:
Four flowers of blood have nailed Him to the walls of Harlem."

Along the white halls of the clinics and the hospitals
Pilate evaporates with a cry:
They have cut down two hundred Judases,
Hanged by the neck in the opera houses and the museum.
Across the cages of the keyless aviaries,
The lines and wires, the gallows of the broken kites,
Crucify, against the fearful light,
The ragged dresses of the little children.   *1946*

HYMN OF NOT MUCH PRAISE FOR NEW YORK CITY

When the windows of the West Side clash like cymbals
     in the setting sunlight,
And when wind wails amid the East Side's aerials,
And when, both north and south of thirty-fourth street,
In all the dizzy buildings,
The elevators clack their teeth and rattle the bars of their cages,
Then the children of the city,
Leaving the monkey-houses of their office-buildings and
     apartments,

With the greatest difficulty open their mouths, and sing:
"Queen among the cities of the Earth: New York!
Rich as a cake, common as a doughnut,
Expensive as a fur and crazy as cocaine,
We love to hear you shake
Your big face like a shining bank
Letting the mad world know you're full of dimes!

"This is your night to make maraccas out of all that metal money
Paris is in the prison-house, and London dies of cancer.
This is the time for you to whirl,
Queen of our hopped-up peace,
And let the excitement of your somewhat crippled congas
Supersede the waltzes of more shining
Capitals that have been bombed.

"Meanwhile we, your children,
Weeping in our seasick zoo of windows while you dance,
Will gobble aspirins,
And try to keep our cage from caving in.
All the while our minds will fill with these petitions,
Flowering quietly in between our gongs of pulse.
These will have to serve as prayers:

"'O lock us in the safe jails of thy movies!
Confine us to the semiprivate wards and white asylums
Of the unbearable cocktail parties, O New York!
Sentence us for life to the penitentiaries of thy bars and night-
      clubs,
And leave us stupefied forever by the blue, objective lights
That fill the pale infirmaries of thy restaurants,
And the clinics of thy schools and offices,
And the operating-rooms of thy dance-halls.

"'But never give us any explanations, even when we ask,
Why all our food tastes of iodoform,

And even the freshest flowers smell of funerals.
No, never let us look about us long enough to wonder
Which of the rich men, shivering in the overheated office,
And which of the poor men, sleeping face-down on the
    Daily Mirror,
Are still alive, and which are dead.'"   *1940–42 {1971}*

FIGURES FOR AN APOCALYPSE

IN THE RUINS OF NEW YORK

The moon is paler than an actress.
We have beheld her mourning in the brown ivy
Of the dendric bridges,—
In the brown, broken ivy
That loves but a span of air.

The moon is paler than an actress, and weeps for you, New York,
Seeking to see you through the tattered bridges,
Leaning down to catch the sham brass
Of your sophisticated voice,
Whose songs are heard no more!

Oh how quiet it is after the black night
When flames out of the clouds burned down your cariated teeth,
And when those lightnings,
Lancing the black boils of Harlem and the Bronx,
Spilled the remaining prisoners,
(The tens and twenties of the living)
Into the trees of Jersey,
To the green farms, to find their liberty.

How are they down, how have they fallen down
Those great strong towers of ice and steel,
And melted by what terror and what miracle?
What fires and lights tore down,
With the white anger of their sudden accusation,
Those towers of silver and of steel?

You whose streets grew up on trellises
With roots in Bowling Green and tap-roots in the Upper Bay:
How are you stripped, now, to your skeleton:

What has become of your live and dead flesh:
Where is the shimmer of your bawdy leaves?
Oh, where your children in the evening of your final Sunday
Gunned after one another in the shadows of the Paramount,
The ashes of the leveled towers still curl with tufts of smoke
Veiling your obsequies in their incinerating haze
They write, in embers, this, your epitaph:

"This was a city
That dressed herself in paper money.
She lived four hundred years
With nickels running in her veins.
She loved the waters of the seven purple seas,
And burned on her own green harbor
Higher and whiter than ever any Tyre.
She was as callous as a taxi;
Her high-heeled eyes were sometimes blue as gin,
And she nailed them, all the days of her life,
Through the hearts of her six million poor.
Now she has died in the terrors of a sudden contemplation
—Drowned in the waters of her own, her poisoned well."

Can we console you, stars,
For the so long survival of such wickedness?
Tomorrow and the day after
Grasses and flowers will grow
Upon the bosom of Manhattan.
And soon the branches of the hickory and sycamore
Will wave where all those dirty windows were—
Ivy and the wild-grape vine
Will tear those weak walls down,
Burying the brownstone fronts in freshness and fragrant flowers;
And the wild-rose and the crab-apple tree
Will bloom in all those silent mid-town dells.

There shall be doves' nests, and hives of bees
In the cliffs of the ancient apartments,

And birds shall sing in the sunny hawthorns
Where was once Park Avenue.
And where Grand Central was, shall be a little hill
Clustered with sweet, dark pine.

Will there be some farmer, think you,
Clearing a place in the woods,
Planting an acre of bannering corn
On the heights above Harlem forest?
Will hunters come explore
The virgin glades of Broadway for the lynx and deer?
Or will some hermit, hiding in the birches, build himself a cell
With the stones of the city hall,
When all the caved-in subways turn to streams
And creeks of fish,
Flowing in sun and silence to the reedy Battery?

But now the moon is paler than a statue.
She reaches out and hangs her lamp
In the iron trees of this destroyed Hesperides.
And by that light, under the caves that once were banks and theaters,
The hairy ones come out to play—
And we believe we hear the singing of the manticores
Echo along the rocks of Wall and Pine

And we are full of fear, and muter than the upside-down stars
That limp in the lame waters,
Muter than the mother moon who, white as death,
Flies and escapes across the wastes of Jersey.

LANDSCAPE: BEAST

Yonder, by the eastward sea
Where smoke melts in a saucer of extinguished cities,
The last men stand, in delegations,

Waiting to see the seven-headed business
Promised us, from those unpublished deeps:
Waiting to see those horns and diadems
And hear the seven voices of the final blasphemy.

And westward, where the other waters are as slick as silk
And slide, in the grey evening, with uncertain lights,
(Screened by the smoke of the extinguished studios)
The last men wait to see the seven-headed thing.
They stand around the radios
Wearing their regalia on their thin excited breasts,
Waving the signals of their masonry.
What will happen, when they see those heads, those horns
Dishevel the flickering sea?

How will they bare their foreheads, and put forth their hands
And wince with the last indelible brand,
And wear the dolour of that animal's number,
And evermore be burned with her disgusting name?

Inland in the lazy distance, where a dozen planes still play
As loud as horseflies, round the ruins of an average town,
A blue-green medium dragon, swimming in the river,
Emerges from the muddy waters, comes to romp awhile
        upon the land.
She rises on the pathless shore,
And goes to roll in the ashes of the ravaged country.
But no man turns to see and be surprised
Where those grey flanks flash palely in the sun.
Who shall gather to see an ordinary dragon, in this day of anger,
Or wonder at those scales as usual as sin?

Meanwhile, upon the broken mountains of the south
No one observes the angels passing to and fro:
And no one sees the fire that shoots beneath the hoofs
Of all the white, impatient horses.

And no one hears or fears the music of those blazing swords.

(Northward, northward, what lies there to see?
Who shall recount the terror of those ruined streets?

And who shall dare to look where all the birds with golden beaks
Stab at the blue eyes of the murdered saints?)

THE HEAVENLY CITY

City, when we see you coming down,
Coming down from God
To be the new world's crown:
How shall they sing, the fresh, unsalted seas
Hearing your harmonies!
For there is no more death,
No need to cure those waters, now, with any brine;
Their shores give them no dead,
Rivers no blood, no rot to stain them.

Because the cruel algebra of war
Is now no more.
And the steel circle of time, inexorable,
Bites like a padlock shut, forever,
In the smoke of the last bomb:
And in that trap the murderers and sorcerers and crooked leaders
Go rolling home to hell.
And history is done.

Shine with your lamb-light, shine upon the world:
You are the new creation's sun.
And standing on their twelve foundations,
Lo, the twelve gates that are One Christ are wide as canticles:
And Oh! Begin to hear the thunder of the songs within
        the crystal Towers,

While all the saints rise from their earth with feet like light
And fly to tread the quick-gold of those streets,

Oh City, when we see you sailing down,
Sailing down from God,
Dressed in the glory of the Trinity, and angel-crowned
In nine white diadems of liturgy.   *1947*

CHRISTOPHER COLUMBUS

There was a great Captain with Mary in his sails
Who did not discover Harlem or the East Side
Or Sing Sing or the dead men on the island.
But his heart was like the high mountains.
And when the king gave him money
To go and discover a country
And fixed him up with robes of gold

He threw down all those pesos and stripped to his champion skin
And waded into the waters of the sea.
The surf boiled white about his knees
And the tides folded behind him
When he caught the furthest caravels and passed them by.
"There goes Columbus! There he goes!" the sailors cried,
Still he is head and shoulders above the horizon
Leaving us like the pillars of Hercules
Standing westward on the way to the Azores!
What land will he find to believe in, now he knows the world
        is round?

Forest upon forest, mile upon empty mile
The undiscovered continent lies, rock upon rock:
The lakes awake, or move in their mute sleep.
Huge rivers wander where the plains
Are cloudy or dark with seas of buffalo.
Frail waterbirds sing in the weeds of Florida.
Northward, grey seas stir
In sight of the unconscious hills.
There are no prints in the thin snows of Maine.

Suddenly the great Christ-bearing Columbus rises in the sea
Spilling the green Atlantic from his shoulders

And sees America through a veil of waters.
Steam things low like cattle all around him in the rivers.
Towers stand like churches on the rock, in a garden of boats;
Citizens look up like snap-dragons
Crowding the streets and galleries and saluting heaven
    with their songs.
Music comes cascading down the stones until all walls
Are singing the feasts of the saints in the light of processions.

Then the discoverer, rising from the harbor,
Taking the river in his stride
Overtops all tall palaces.
The people cheer their noon-day sun, their giant Gospel
And calm Columbus reaches down to the citizens
The golden fruits of which his arms are full.

All over the new land woods retire to the hills.
Indians come out of the brake with corn and melons
And he blesses the bronze gentry sitting in the air of the arcade:
Thousands of Franciscans go through the fields with Sacraments
And towns, towns, towns rise out of the ground.

Then the Americans, wearing the new names of saints
Look up and sing into the face of their tall Father
While he is lifted from the earth, blesses his continent.
Birds fly like language from the cloud, his beard.

His smiles are quickly muffled in the sky.
His gestures mild, they melt and disappear.
Waving, waving the little ones have wept him out of sight.

When it is evening, in America's vespers
Feathers of imperfect incense spend themselves
Marking his memory on steeples.
As fast as dark comes down towns, cities,

Returning to the virgin air
Restore these shores to silences.
Woods crawl back into the gulf.
Shadows of Franciscans die in tangled wilds
And there is just one smoke upon the plain
And just one Indian hunter.

What will you do tomorrow, America
Found and lost so soon?
Your Christ has died and gone to Spain
Bearing a precious cross upon his shoulder
And there your story lies in chains.

But the devils are sailing for your harbors
Launching their false doves into the air to fly for your sands.
They bend over their tillers with little fox faces,
Grin like dollars through their fur,
And their meat-eating sails fly down and fold upon your shore.

Suddenly the silences of the deep continent
Die in a tornado of guitars.
Our own America tears down her mask of trees
Hailing each pirate with sarcastic towns.
Break open a dozen cities! Let traffic bleed upon the land
And hug your hundred and twenty million paupers in a vice
        without escape
While they are mapped and verified
Plotted, printed, catalogued, numbered and categoried
And sold to the doctors of your sham discovery.

✛

And now the cities' eyes are tight as ice
When the long cars stream home in nights of autumn.
(The bells Columbus heard are dumb.)
The city's rivers are as still as liquor.

Bars and factories pool their lights
In Michigan's or Erie's mirrors, now, on the night of the game.
(But the bells Columbus heard are dumb.)
The city's face is frozen like a screen of silver
When the universities turn in
And winter sings in the bridges
Tearing the grand harps down.

But the children sing no hymn for the feast of Saint Columbus.
They watch the long, long armies drifting home.   *1949*

THE GUNS OF FORT KNOX

Guns at the camp (I hear them suddenly)
Guns make the little houses jump. I feel
Explosions in my feet, through boards.
Wars work under the floor. Wars
Dance in the foundations. Trees
Must also feel the guns they do not want
Even in their core.
As each charge bumps the shocked earth
They shudder from the root.

Shock the hills, you guns! They are
Not too firm even without dynamite.
These Chinese clayfoot hills
Founded in their own shale
Shift their feet in friable stone.

        Such ruins cannot
Keep the armies of the dead
From starting up again.

They'll hear these guns tonight
Tomorrow or some other time.
They'll wake. They'll rise
Through the stunned rocks, form
Regiments and do death's work once more.

Guns, I say, this is not
The right resurrection. All day long
You punch the doors of death to wake
A slain generation. Let them lie
Still. Let them sleep on,
O Guns. Shake no more
(But leave the locks secure)
Hell's door.   *1957*

DARJEELING

And to dissolve the heaps. Afternoon lumber water filling
can full
Taxi call kids. Sharp cries spread rev motor whisper pony feet
        Hoo! Hoo!
Motor going gone (hill)
Looking back her long hair shining pattern of crosses
        unionjacks
shadows on the walk (Hoo! Hoo! Ponyfeet)
Ponysaddle afternoon all rich god Ganesha fills his waterpot.
All to dissolve the lagers (layers) spreads of sounds—waters,
        boards, planks, plankfall fur, voice near, man holds
        basket of green leaves. Going. Gone.
Sensations neutral low degree burn (sun) warmskin. Hears a little
water,
Again fills watercan the poor one—not rich Ganesha, he is
        gone in scarf

and glasses.
All come worship fun in the sun.
And to dissolve the fun. Worker basket empty and gone.
    Ganesha
gone in an
Oxblood muffler though not cold after good hot dinner
All come have fun dissolve values. Tibetan boss explains garden.
Layers of sounds hammer upon the ear spread selves away rich
roaring bark (spurs values) menaces bishop (Distances)
Image yards. Bogus is this freight!
Gate measure stransound gone taxi Water whumps in can
and fills softer, softer, gone of hearing.
Dog is crazy angry barkleap fighting any wires.
Gone basket of foliage
Bangs on an old bucket. *Inutile!*
Motorbike argues with some slops. Taxicry downhill in small
city. Outcry!
Disarms v. chords.
Image yards spread wide open
Eye tracks work their way everywhere.
Mountain winds can harm voice.
Sensation neutral low four o'clock tone is general. Must call
a nun on the telephone.
Two bad cheers for the small sun: burning a little
life sunstorm: is not yet overcloudy winter!
Send aid ideas to dissolve heaps—to spread their freight.   *1977*

Songs of Experience; India, One

(Poem and Prayer to Golden Expensive Mother Oberoi)

O thou Mother Oberoi
Crosseyed goddess of death
Showing your blue tongue
Dancing upon Shiva or someone
With sharks in front gas—
Tanks empty the ambassadors
Coming tonight they
Shine you up
You Intercon—
Tinental Mam—
Moth   Mother Kali Con—
Crete Oberoi not yet
Stained with the greygreen
Aftermoss of the monsoons
And a big clean pool
(Shacks out front and kids
In the red-flowers and
Goats) a big clean pool I say
With one American
General Motors type
Doing a slow breast-
Stroke in the chlorinated
Indigo water where no
Slate-blue buffalo has ever
Got wet
O thou merciful naked
Jumping millionaire
Rich in skeletons and buffets
You have taken
All our money away
Wearing a precious collar

Of men's heads
(Those blacks love you at night
In a trance of drums
Sitting with red headlights
Between their eyebrows)
With shacks out front
When kids are playing
With dusty asses
In scarlet flowers
While on your immaculate
Carpets all the am-
Bassadors from General Electric
Slowly chase their bluehaired wives
In high-heeled sneakers.   *1977*

TWO

POEMS FROM THE MONASTERY

HOLY COMMUNION: THE CITY

"What light will, in your eyes, like an archangel,
Soon stand armed,
O you who come with looks more lowly than the dewy valleys,
And kneel like lepers on the step of Bethlehem?

"Although we know no hills, no country rivers,
Here in the jungles of our waterpipes and iron ladders,
Our thoughts are quieter than rivers,
Our loves are simpler than the trees,
Our prayers deeper than the sea.

"What wounds had furrowed up our dry and fearful spirit
Until the massbells came like rain to make them vineyards?

"Now, brighter on our minds' bright mountains
Than the towns of Israel,
Shall shine desire!

"O Glory, be not swift to vanish like the wine's slight savor,
And still lie lightly, Truth, upon our tongues,
For Grace moves, like the wind,
The armies of the wheat our secret hero!
And Faith sits in our hearts like fire,
And makes them smile like suns,

"While we come back from lovely Bethlehem
To burn down Harlem with the glad Word of Our Saviour."

1944

THE TRAPPIST ABBEY: MATINS

(OUR LADY OF GETHSEMANI, KENTUCKY)

When the full fields begin to smell of sunrise
And the valleys sing in their sleep,
The pilgrim moon pours over the solemn darkness
Her waterfalls of silence,
And then departs, up the long avenue of trees.

The stars hide, in the glade, their light, like tears,
And tremble where some train runs, lost,
Baying in eastward mysteries of distance,
Where fire flares, somewhere, over a sink of cities.

Now kindle in the windows of this ladyhouse, my soul,
Your childish, clear awakeness:
Burn in the country night
Your wise and sleepless lamp.
For, from the frowning tower, the windy belfry,
Sudden the bells come, bridegrooms,
And fill the echoing dark with love and fear.

Wake in the windows of Gethsemani, my soul, my sister,
For the past years, with smokey torches, come,
Bringing betrayal from the burning world
And bloodying the glade with pitch flame.

Wake in the cloisters of the lonely night, my soul, my sister,
Where the apostles gather, who were, one time, scattered,
And mourn God's blood in the place of His betrayal,
And weep with Peter at the triple cock-crow.   *1944*

The Blessed Virgin Mary Compared to a Window

Because my will is simple as a window
And knows no pride of original earth,
It is my life to die, like glass, by light:
Slain in the strong rays of the bridegroom sun.

Because my love is simple as a window
And knows no shame of original dust,
I longed all night, (when I was visible) for dawn my death:
When I would marry day, my Holy Spirit:
And die by transsubstantiation into light.

For light, my lover, steals my life in secret.
I vanish into day, and leave no shadow
But the geometry of my cross,
Whose frame and structure are the strength
By which I die, but only to the earth,
And am uplifted to the sky my life.

When I become the substance of my lover,
(Being obedient, sinless glass)
I love all things that need my lover's life,
And live to give my newborn Morning to your quiet rooms,

—Your rooms, that would be tombs,
Or vaults of night, and death, and terror,
Fill with the clarity of living Heaven,
Shine with the rays of God's Jerusalem:
O shine, bright Sions!

Because I die by brightness and the Holy Spirit,
The sun rejoices in your jail, my kneeling Christian,
(Where even now you weep and grin
To learn, from my simplicity, the strength of faith.)

Therefore do not be troubled at the judgments of the thunder.
Stay still and pray, still stay, my other son,
And do not fear the armies and black ramparts
Of the advancing and retreating rains:
I'll let no lightning kill your room's white order.

Although it is the day's last hour,
Look with no fear:
For the torn storm lets in, at the world's rim,
Three streaming rays as straight as Jacob's ladder:

And you shall see the sun, my Son, my Substance,
Come to convince the world of the day's end, and of the night,
Smile to the lovers of the day in smiles of blood:
For through my love, He'll be their Brother,
My light—the Lamb of their Apocalypse.   *1944*

How Long We Wait

How long we wait, with minds as quiet as time,
Like sentries on a tower.
How long we watch, by night, like the astronomers.

Heaven, when will we hear you sing,
Arising from our grassy hills,
And say: "The dark is done, and Day
Laughs like a Bridegroom in His tent, the lovely sun,
His tent the sun, His tent the smiling sky!"

How long we wait with minds as dim as ponds
While stars swim slowly homeward in the water of our west!
Heaven, when will we hear you sing?

How long we listened to the silence of our vineyards
And heard no bird stir in the rising barley.
The stars go home behind the shaggy trees.
Our minds are grey as rivers.

O earth, when will you wake in the green wheat,
And all our Trappist cedars sing:
"Bright land, lift up your leafy gates!
You abbey steeple, sing with bells!
For look, our Sun rejoices like a dancer
On the rim of our hills."

In the blue west the moon is uttered like the word:
    "Farewell."   *1946*

A LETTER TO MY FRIENDS

ON ENTERING THE MONASTERY OF OUR LADY OF GETHSEMANI, 1941

This holy House of God,
Nazareth, where Christ lived as a boy,
These sheds and cloisters,
The very stones and beams are all befriended
By cleaner sun, by rarer birds, by lovelier flowers.

Lost in the tigers' and the lions' wilderness,
More than we fear, we love these holy stones,
These thorns, the phoenix's sweet and spikey tree.

More than we fear, we love the holy desert,
Where separate strangers, hid in their disguises,
Have come to meet, by night, the quiet Christ.

We who have some time wandered in those crowded ruins,
(Farewell, you woebegone, sad towns)
We who have wandered like (the ones I hear) the moaning trains,
(Begone, sad towns!)
We'll live it over for you here.

Here all your ruins are rebuilt as fast as you destroy yourselves,
In your unlucky wisdom,
Here in the House of God
And on the holy hill,
Where fields are the friends of plenteous heaven,
While starlight feeds, as bright as manna,
All our rough earth with wakeful grace.

And look, the ruins have become Jerusalems,
And the sick cities re-arise, like shining Sions!
Jerusalems, these walls and rooves,
These bowers and fragrant sheds,
Our desert's wooden door,
The arches, and the windows, and the tower!   *1946*

TRAPPISTS, WORKING

Now all our saws sing holy sonnets in this world of timber
Where oaks go off like guns, and fall like cataracts,
Pouring their roar into the wood's green well.

Walk to us, Jesus, through the wall of trees,
And find us still adorers in these airy churches,
Singing our other Office with our saws and axes.
Still teach Your children in the busy forest,
And let some little sunlight reach us, in our mental shades,
    and leafy studies.

When time has turned the country white with grain
And filled our regions with the thrashing sun,
Walk to us, Jesus, through the walls of wheat
When our two tractors come to cut them down:
Sow some light winds upon the acres of our spirit,
And cool the regions where our prayers are reapers,
And slake us, Heaven, with Your living rivers.   *1946*

AFTER THE NIGHT OFFICE—GETHSEMANI ABBEY

It is not yet the grey and frosty time
When barns ride out of the night like ships:
We do not see the Brothers, bearing lanterns,
Sink in the quiet mist,
As various as the spirits who, with lamps, are sent
To search our souls' Jerusalems
Until our houses are at rest
And minds enfold the Word, our Guest.

Praises and canticles anticipate
Each day the singing bells that wake the sun,
But now our psalmody is done.
Our hasting souls outstrip the day:
Now, before dawn, they have their noon.
The Truth that transsubstantiates the body's night
Has made our minds His temple-tent:
Open the secret eye of faith
And drink these deeps of invisible light.

The weak walls
Of the world fall
And heaven, in floods, comes pouring in:

Sink from your shallows, soul, into eternity,
And slake your wonder at that deep-lake spring.
We touch the rays we cannot see,
We feel the light that seems to sing.

Go back to bed, red sun, you are too late,
And hide behind Mount Olivet—
For like the flying moon, held prisoner,
Within the branches of a juniper,
So in the cages of consciousness
The Dove of God is prisoner yet:
Unruly sun, go back to bed.

But now the lances of the morning
Fire all their gold against the steeple and the water-tower.
Returning to the windows of our deep abode of peace,
Emerging at our conscious doors
We find our souls all soaked in grace, like Gideon's fleece.

1946

THE TRAPPIST CEMETERY—GETHSEMANI

Brothers, the curving grasses and their daughters
Will never print your praises:
The trees our sisters, in their summer dresses,
Guard your fame in these green cradles:
The simple crosses are content to hide your characters.

Oh do not fear
The birds that bicker in the lonely belfry
Will ever give away your legends.
Yet when the sun, exulting like a dying martyr,
Canonizes, with his splendid fire, the sombre hills,

Your graves all smile like little children,
And your wise crosses trust the mothering night
That folds them in the Sanctuary's wings.

You need not hear the momentary rumors of the road
Where cities pass and vanish in a single car
Filling the cut beside the mill
With roar and radio,
Hurling the air into the wayside branches
Leaving the leaves alive with panic.

See, the kind universe,
Wheeling in love about the abbey steeple,
Lights up your sleepy nursery with stars.

✢

God, in your bodily life,
Untied the snares of anger and desire,
Hid your flesh from envy by these country altars,
Beneath these holy eaves where even sparrows have their houses.
But oh, how like the swallows and the chimney swifts
Do your free souls in glory play!
And with a cleaner flight,
Keener, more graceful circles,
Rarer and finer arcs
Then all these innocent attacks that skim our steeple!
How like these children of the summer evening
Do your rejoicing spirits
Deride the dry earth with their aviation!

But now the treble harps of night begin to play in the deep wood,
To praise your holy sleep,
And all the frogs along the creek
Chant in the moony waters to the Queen of Peace.
And we, the mariners, and travellers,

The wide-eyed immigrants,
Praying and sweating in our steerage cabins,
Lie still and count with love the measured bells
That tell the deep-sea leagues until your harbor.

Already on this working earth you knew what nameless love
Adorns the heart with peace by night,
Hearing, adoring all the dark arrivals of eternity.
Oh, here on earth you knew what secret thirst
Arming the mind with instinct,
Answers the challenges of God with garrisons
Of unified desire
And facing Him in His new wars
Is slain at last in an exchange of lives.

Teach us, Cistercian Fathers, how to wear
Silence, our humble armor.
Pray us a torrent of the seven spirits
That are our wine and stamina:
Because your work is not yet done.
But look: the valleys shine with promises,
And every burning morning is a prophecy of Christ
Coming to raise and vindicate
Even our sorry flesh.

Then will your graves, Gethsemani, give up their angels,
Return them to their souls to learn
The songs and attitudes of glory.
Then will creation rise again like gold
Clean, from the furnace of your litanies:
The beasts and trees shall share your resurrection,
And a new world be born from these green tombs.   *1946*

POEM IN THE RAIN AND THE SUN

Watching the world from my peeled doorlight
Without my rain or my shame
My noonday dusk made steps upon the rock:
Tall drops pelted the steps with black jewels
Belonging to the old world's bones.

Owning the view in the air of a hermit's weather
I counted the fragmentary rain
In drops as blue as coal
Until I plumbed the shadows full of thunder.
My prayers supervised the full-armed atmosphere
And storms called all hounds home.

Then out of the towering water
Four or five mountains came walking
To see the chimneys of the little graves.
Flying the neutral stones I dwelt beneath the pines
And saw the countries sleeping in their beds,
Lands of the watermen, where the poplars bend.
Wild seas amuse the world with water:
No end to the surfs that charm our altars
And fatten the wide sands with their old foam and their old roar.

Thus in the boom of the wave's advantage
Dogs and lions come to my tame home
Won by the bells of this Cistercian jungle,
Where waves slow down their silence at my feet:
O love the livid fringes
In which their robes are drenched:

Songs of the lions and whales!
With my pen between my fingers,

Making the waterworld sing.
Sweet Christ, discover diamonds
And sapphires in my verse
While I burn the sap of my pine house
For the praise of the ocean sun!

I have walked upon the surf
Rinsing the bays with Thy hymns
My prayers have swept the horizons clean
Of ships and rain.
All the waters are slick as lacquer.
Upon these polished swells my feet no longer run:
Sliding all over the waves I come
To the hope of a slippery harbor.

The dogs have gone back to their ghosts
And the many lions, home.
But words fling wide the windows of their glassy houses—

Then Adam and Eve come out and walk along the coast
Praising the tears of the sun
While I am decorating with Thy rubies the bones
    of the autumn trees,
The bones of the homecoming world.   *1949*

SPRING: MONASTERY FARM

When it is spring,
When the huge bulls roam in their pens
And sing like trains;
When the white orchards dream in the noon
And all those trees are dens of light
And boom with honey bees,

The blue-eyed streams
No longer lock their mirth among the icy shales
But run to meet the sun with faces clean.

When Aries
Stands at the crossed ecliptic with a golden cry,
We'll sing the grain that dies and triumphs in the secret ground.
Though in our labor and our rational Lent we bend our heads
And glaze the dark earth with a shining ploughshare,
Our minds more ardent, hearts insatiable
Than all the amber bees that wrestle in the daffodils,
Sing in the flowers of Your theology.

For, in the sap and music of the region's spring
We hear the picture of Your voice, Creator,
And in our heartspeace answer You
And offer You the world.

For, for all these, their spring is their necessity:
But we have traded April for our ransom and our Hundredfold.
Our songs complete those deep, uncomprehending choirs.

For, for all these, their spring is their necessity,
Which, by Your Cross and grace, is made our glory and our
      Sacrament:
As every golden instant mints the Christ Who keeps us free.

1947

THE READER

Lord, when the clock strikes
Telling the time with cold tin
And I sit hooded in this lectern

Waiting for the monks to come,
I see the red cheeses, and bowls
All smile with milk in ranks upon their tables.

Light fills my proper globe
(I have won light to read by
With a little, tinkling chain)

And the monks come down the cloister
With robes as voluble as water.
I do not see them but I hear their waves.

It is winter, and my hands prepare
To turn the pages of the saints:
And to the trees Thy moon has frozen on the windows
My tongue shall sing Thy Scripture.

Then the monks pause upon the step
(With me here in this lectern
And Thee there on Thy crucifix)
And gather little pearls of water on their fingers' ends
Smaller than this my psalm.   *1949*

ON A DAY IN AUGUST

These woods are too impersonal.
The deaf-and-dumb fields, waiting to be shaved of hay
Suffer the hours like an unexpected sea
While locusts fry their music in the sycamores.

But from the curdled places of the sky
(Where a brown wing hovers for carrion)

We have not seen the heaven-people come.
The clean, white saints, have they forgotten us?
Here we lie upon the earth
In the air of our dead grove
Dreaming some wind may come and kiss ourselves in the red eyes
With a pennyworth of mercy for our pepper shoulders.
And so we take into our hands the ruins
Of the words our minds have rent.

It is enough.
Our souls are trying to crawl out of our pores.
Our lives are seeping through each part of us like vinegar.
A sad sour death is eating the roots of our hair.

Yet doors of sanitary winds lie open in the clouds
To vistas of those laundries where the clean saints dwell:
If we could only view them from our slum!
But our dream has wandered away
And drowned in the din of the crickets' disconnected prayer.

Thus the grasses and the unemployed goldenrod
Go revel through our farm, and dance around the field.
The blue-black lights come shimmering upon the tar
Where kids made footprints in the melting way to Louisville.
And spooks come out of the road and walk the jagged heat
Like the time we found that drunkard lying still as murder
In the ditch behind the mill.

But you, Saint Clare,
We have been looking up your stairs all afternoon
Wanting to see you walking down some nimbus
          with your gentle friends.

Very well, clouds,
Open your purple bottles,

Cozen us never more with blowsy cotton:
But organize,
Summon the punishing lightning:
Spring those sudden gorgeous trees against the dark
Curtain of apocalypse you'll hang to earth, from heaven:
Let five white branches scourge the land with fire!
And when the first fat drops
Spatter upon the tin top of our church like silver dollars
And thoughts come bathing back to mind with a new life,
Prayer will become our new discovery

When God and His bad earth once more make friends.   *1949*

ELEGY FOR THE MONASTERY BARN

As though an aged person were to wear
Too gay a dress
And walk about the neighborhood
Announcing the hour of her death,

So now, one summer day's end,
At suppertime, when wheels are still,
The long barn suddenly puts on the traitor, beauty,
And hails us with a dangerous cry,
For: "Look!" she calls to the country,
"Look how fast I dress myself in fire!"

Had we half guessed how long her spacious shadows
Harbored a woman's vanity
We would be less surprised to see her now
So loved, and so attended, and so feared.

She, in whose airless heart
We burst our veins to fill her full of hay,
Now stands apart.
She will not have us near her. Terribly,
Sweet Christ, how terribly her beauty burns us now!

And yet she has another legacy,
More delicate, to leave us, and more rare.

Who knew her solitude?
Who heard the peace downstairs
While flames ran whispering among the rafters?
Who felt the silence, there,
The long, hushed gallery
Clean and resigned and waiting for the fire?

Look! They have all come back to speak their summary:
Fifty invisible cattle, the past years
Assume their solemn places one by one.
This is the little minute of their destiny.
Here is their meaning found. Here is their end.

Laved in the flame as in a Sacrament
The brilliant walls are holy
In their first-last hour of joy.

Fly from within the barn! Fly from the silence
Of this creature sanctified by fire!
Let no man stay inside to look upon the Lord!
Let no man wait within and see the Holy
One sitting in the presence of disaster
Thinking upon this barn His gentle doom!   *1957*

SOLITARY LIFE

White-collar man blue-collar
Man I am a no-collar man
(least of all a *Roman* collar!)
Shave twice a week
Maybe.

Hear the trains out there
Two miles away
Trucks too
The road not near.

Hear the owls in the wood and pray
When I can
I don't talk
About all that
What is there to say?

Yes, I had beer in this place
A while back and once
Whiskey.

And I worry about the abbot
Coming up here to
Inspect
And finding
A copy of *Newsweek*
Under the bed.

Now it's another
Morning and the doves
Boom softly and the world
Goes on it seems
Forever.

1963

ELEGY FOR A TRAPPIST

Maybe the martyrology until today
Has found no fitting word to describe you
Confessor of exotic roses
Martyr of unbelievable gardens

Whom we will always remember
As a tender-hearted careworn
Generous unsteady cliff
Lurching in the cloister
Like a friendly freight train
To some uncertain station

Master of the sudden enthusiastic gift
In an avalanche
Of flower catalogues
And boundless love.

Sometimes a little dangerous at corners
Vainly trying to smuggle
Some enormous and perfect bouquet
To a side altar
In the sleeves of your cowl

In the dark before dawn
On the day of your burial
A big truck with lights
Moved like a battle cruiser
Toward the gate
Past your abandoned and silent garden

The brief glare
Lit up the grottos, pyramids and presences

One by one
Then the gate swung red
And clattered shut in the giant lights
And everything was gone

As if Leviathan
Hot on the scent of some other blood
Had passed you by
And never saw you hiding in the flowers.   *1977*

MERLIN AND THE DEER

After thrashing in the water of the reservoir
The deer swims beautifully
And so escapes
Limping across the country road into the little cedars.

Followed by Merlin's eye
Bewitched, a simple spirit
Merlin awakes
He becomes a gentle savage
Dressed in leaves
He hums alone in the glade
Says only a few phrases to himself
Or a psalm to his companion
Light in the wood.

Yes they can kill
The lovely doe and deer
In and out of season.

And messengers also
Come to bring him back
To hours and offices of men.

But he sees again
The curved and graceful deer
Fighting in the water
And then leaving

So he pulls out
Of all that icy water himself
And leaves the people

"Il revient à ses forêts
Et cette fois pour toujours."

Now caught in many spells
Willing prisoner of trees and rain
And magic blossoms
The invisible people

Visit his jail
With forest stories
Tales without sound
And without conclusion
Clear fires without smoke
Fumbled prophecies
And Celtic fortunes.   *1977*

THE OLD MONK IS TURNED LOOSE

The old monk is turned loose
And can travel!
He's out to see the world.
What progress in the last thirty years!
But his mode of travel
Is still the same.   *1977*

A Practical Program for Monks

1

Each one shall sit at table with his own cup and spoon, and with
    his own repentance. Each one's own business shall be his most
    important affair, and provide his own remedies.
They have neglected bowl and plate.
Have you a wooden fork?
Yes, each monk has a wooden fork as well as a potato.

2

Each one shall wipe away tears with his own saint, when three
    bells hold in store a hot afternoon. Each one is supposed to
    mind his own heart, with its conscience, night and morning.
Another turn on the wheel: ho hum! And observe the Abbot!
Time to go to bed in a straw blanket.

3

Plenty of bread for everyone between prayers and the psalter:
    will you recite another?
Merci, and *Miserere.*
Always mind both the clock and the Abbot until eternity.
Miserere.

4

Details of the Rule are all liquid and solid. What canon was the
    first to announce regimentation before us? Mind the step on
    the way down!
Yes, I dare say you are right, Father. I believe you; I believe you.
I believe it is easier when they have ice water and even a lemon.
Each one can sit at table with his own lemon, and mind his
    conscience.

5

Can we agree that the part about the lemon is regular?

In any case, it is better to have sheep than peacocks, and cows rather than a chained leopard says Modest, in one of his proverbs.

The monastery, being owner of a communal rowboat, is the antechamber of heaven.

Surely that ought to be enough.

6

Each one can have some rain after Vespers on a hot afternoon, but *ne quid nimis,* or the purpose of the Order will be forgotten.

We shall send you hyacinths and a sweet millennium.

Everything the monastery provides is very pleasant to see and to sell for nothing.

What is baked smells fine. There is a sign of God on every leaf that nobody sees in the garden. The fruit trees are there on purpose, even when no one is looking. Just put the apples in the basket.

In Kentucky there is also room for a little cheese.

Each one shall fold his own napkin, and neglect the others.

7

Rain is always very silent in the night, under such gentle cathedrals.

Yes, I have taken care of the lamp. *Miserere.*

Have you a patron saint, and an angel?

Thank you. Even though the nights are never dangerous, I have one of everything.

1977

THREE

POEMS OF THE SACRED

SONG

(FROM CROSSPORTION'S PASTORAL)

The bottom of the sea has come
And builded in my noiseless room
The fishes' and the mermaids' home,

Whose it is most, most hell to be
Out of the heavy-hanging sea
And in the thin, thin changeable air

Or unroom sleep some other where;
But play their coral violins
Where waters most lock music in:

The bottom of my room, the sea.
Full of voiceless curtaindeep
There mermaid somnambules come sleep
Where fluted half-lights show the way,

And there, there lost orchestras play
And down the many quarterlights come
To the dim mirth of my aquadrome:
The bottom of my sea, the room.   *1946*

SACRED HEART 2

(A FRAGMENT—)

Geography comes to an end,
Compass has lost all earthly north,
Horizons have no meaning
Nor roads an explanation:

I cannot even hope for any special borealis
To rouse my darkness with a brief "Hurray"!

O flaming Heart,
Unseen and unimagined in this wilderness,
You, You alone are real, and here I've found You.
Here will I love and praise You in a tongueless death,
Until my white devoted bones,
Long bleached and polished by the winds of this Sahara,
Relive at Your command,
Rise and unfold the flowers of their everlasting spring.

                                        1940–42 {1971}

THE WINTER'S NIGHT

When, in the dark, the frost cracks on the window
The children awaken, and whisper.
One says the moonlight grated like a skate
Across the freezing river.
Another hears the starlight breaking like a knifeblade
Upon the silent, steelbright pond.
They say the trees are stiller than the frozen water
From waiting for a shouting light, a heavenly message.

Yet it is far from Christmas, when a star
Sang in the pane, as brittle as their innocence!
For now the light of early Lent
Glitters upon the icy step—
"We have wept letters to our patron saints,
(The children say) yet slept before they ended."

Oh, is there in this night no sound of strings, of singers?
None coming from the wedding, no, nor Bridegroom's messenger?
(The sleepy virgins stir, and trim their lamps.)

The moonlight rings upon the ice as sudden as a footstep;
Starlight clinks upon the dooryard stone, too like a latch,
And the children are, again, awake,
And all call out in whispers to their guardian angels.   *1944*

THE VINE

When wind and winter turn our vineyard
To a bitter Calvary,
What hands come out and crucify us
Like the innocent vine?

How long will starlight weep as sharp as thorns
In the night of our desolate life?
How long will moonlight fear to free the naked prisoner?
Or is there no deliverer?

A mob of winds, on Holy Thursday, come like murderers
And batter the walls of our locked and terrified souls.
Our doors are down, and our defense is done.
Good Friday's rains, in Roman order,
March, with sharpest lances, up our vineyard hill.

More dreadful than St. Peter's cry
When he was being swallowed in the sea,
Cries out our anguish: "O! We are abandoned!"
When in our life we see the ruined vine
Cut open by the cruel spring,
Ploughed by the furious season!

As if we had forgotten how the whips of winter
And the cross of April

Would all be lost in one bright miracle.
For look! The vine on Calvary is bright with branches!
See how the leaves laugh in the light,
And how the whole hill smiles with flowers:
And know how all our numbered veins must run
With life, like the sweet vine, when it is full of sun.   *1944*

THE BIOGRAPHY

Oh read the verses of the loaded scourges,
And what is written in their terrible remarks:
"The Blood runs down the walls of Cambridge town,
As useless as the waters of the narrow river—
While pub and alley gamble for His vesture."

Although my life is written on Christ's Body like a map,
The nails have printed in those open hands
More than the abstract names of sins,
More than the countries and the towns,
The names of streets, the numbers of the houses,
The record of the days and nights,
When I have murdered Him in every square and street.

Lance and thorn, and scourge and nail
Have more than made His Flesh my chronicle.
My journeys more than bite His bleeding feet.

Christ, from my cradle, I had known You everywhere,
And even though I sinned, I walked in You, and knew You were
          my world:
You were my France and England,
My seas and my America:

You were my life and air, and yet I would not own You.

Oh, when I loved You, even while I hated You,
Loving and yet refusing You in all the glories of Your universe

It was Your living Flesh I tore and trampled, not the air and earth:
Not that You feel us, in created things,
But knowing You, in them, made every sin a sacrilege;
And every act of greed became a desecration,
Spoiled and dishonored You as in Your Eucharist.

And yet with every wound You robbed me of a crime,
And as each blow was paid with Blood,
You paid me also each great sin with greater graces.
For even as I killed You,
You made Yourself a greater thief than any in Your company,
Stealing my sins into Your dying life,
Robbing me even of my death.

Where, on what cross my agony will come
I do not ask You:
For it is written and accomplished here,
On every Crucifix, on every altar.
It is my narrative that drowns and is forgotten
In Your five open Jordans,
Your voice that cries my: *"Consummatum est."*

If on Your Cross Your life and death and mine are one,
Love teaches me to read, in You, the rest of a new history.
I trace my days back to another childhood,
Exchanging, as I go,
New York and Cuba for Your Galilee,
And Cambridge for Your Nazareth,
Until I come again to my beginning,
And find a manger, star and straw,

A pair of animals, some simple men,
And thus I learn that I was born,
Now not in France, but Bethlehem.   *1946*

ADVENT

Charm with your stainlessness these winter nights,
Skies, and be perfect!
Fly vivider in the fiery dark, you quiet meteors,
And disappear.
You moon, be slow to go down,
This is your full!

The four white roads make off in silence
Towards the four parts of the starry universe.
Time falls like manna at the corners of the wintry earth.
We have become more humble than the rocks,
More wakeful than the patient hills.

Charm with your stainlessness these nights in Advent, holy spheres,
While minds, as meek as beasts,
Stay close at home in the sweet hay;
And intellects are quieter than the flocks that feed by starlight.

Oh pour your darkness and your brightness over all
       our solemn valleys,
You skies: and travel like the gentle Virgin,
Toward the planets' stately setting,

Oh white full moon as quiet as Bethlehem!   *1946*

CAROL

Flocks feed by darkness with a noise of whispers,
In the dry grass of pastures,
And lull the solemn night with their weak bells.

The little towns upon the rocky hills
Look down as meek as children:
Because they have seen come this holy time.

God's glory, now, is kindled gentler than low candlelight
Under the rafters of a barn:
Eternal Peace is sleeping in the hay,
And Wisdom's born in secret in a straw-roofed stable.

And O! Make holy music in the stars, you happy angels.
You shepherds, gather on the hill.
Look up, you timid flocks, where the three kings
Are coming through the wintry trees;

While we unnumbered children of the wicked centuries
Come after with our penances and prayers,
And lay them down in the sweet-smelling hay
Beside the wise men's golden jars.   *1946*

ASH WEDNESDAY

The naked traveller,
Stretching, against the iron dawn, the bowstrings of his eyes,
Starves on the mad sierra.

But the sleepers,
Prisoners in a lovely world of weeds,
Make a small, red cry,
And change their dreams.

Proud as the mane of the whinnying air,
Yet humble as the flakes of water
Or the chips of the stone sun, the traveller
Is nailed to the hill by the light of March's razor;

And when the desert barks, in a rage of love
For the noon of the eclipse,
He lies with his throat cut, in a frozen crater.

Then the sleepers,
Prisoners of a moonward power of tides,
Slain by the stillness of their own reflections,
Sit up, in their graves, with a white cry,
And die of terror at the traveller's murder.   *1946*

On the Anniversary of My Baptism

Certain waters are as blue as metal
Or as salt as sorrow.
Others wince like brass in the hammering sun,
Or stammer all over with tremors of shadow
That die as fast as the light winds
Whose flights surprise the promontories
And the marble bay.

Some are crowded everywhere, off-shore, with purple coral
Between the fleets of light that founder in the sand.

Others are full of yawls, or loud with launches,
Or sadder than the bitter smoke
Of tug and trawler, tramp and collier,

Or as grey as battle.

Oh! Since I was a baby in the Pyrenees,
When old St. Martin marked me for the cloister from high
    Canigou,

How many deeps, how many wicked seas
Went to befriend me with a flash of white-caps
Louder than laughter in the wind and sun,
Or sluggered all our brown bows gunwale-under
In their rowdy thunder—
Only to return me to the land.

Do you suppose that if the green Atlantic
Had ever cracked our brittle shell
And rifled all the cabins for their fruit of drunken passengers,
Do you suppose my sins,
Once we were sorted and disposed forever
Along the shelves of that profound, unvisited museum,
Would there have been immune,
Or learned to keep their coats of unreality
From the deep sea's most patient candying?

The day You made the waters,
And dragged them down from the dividing islands
And made them spring with fish,
You planned to bless the brine out of the seas
That were to be my death.

And this is the ninth November since my world's end
    and my Genesis,

When, with the sting of salt in my dry mouth,
Cross-crowned with water by the priest,
Stunned at the execution of my old companion, death,
And with the murder of my savage history,
You drowned me in the shallow font.

My eyes, swimming in unexpected infancy,
Were far too frail for such a favor:
They still close-kept the stone shell of their empty sepulchre:
But, though they saw none, guessed the new-come Trinity
That charged my sinews with His secret life.   *1947*

THEORY OF PRAYER

Not in the streets, not in the white streets
Nor in the crowded porticoes
Shall we catch You in our words,
Or lock You in the lenses of our cameras,
You Who escaped the subtle Aristotle,
Blinding us by Your evidence,
Your too clear evidence, Your everywhere.

Not in the groves, not in the flowering green groves
Where the pretty idols dwell
Shall we find the path to Your pavilion
Tented in clouds and fire:—
We are only following the echo
Of our own lyres.

The wise man's blood
Freezes in every vein and artery
With the blue poison of his own indelible prudence.

And the lover,
Caught in the loop of his own lie
Strangles like a hare:
While the singers are suddenly killed,
Slain by the blades of their own song—
The words that clash like razors in the throat
Severing the tender strings.

For the things that we utter turn and betray us,
Writing the names of our sins on flesh and bone
In lights as hard as diamonds.
And the things we think have sold us to the enemy
Writing the names of our sins on the raw marrow
In lights as sharp as glass.
And our desires,
Uncovering their faces one by one
Are seen to be our murderers!
How did you break your jails, you black assassins?
How did you find us out, you numbered men?

Logic has ruined us,
Theorems have flung their folly at us,
Economy has left us full of swords
And all our blood is gone:
Oh, how like a death, now, is our prayer become!
We lie and wait upon the unknown Savior
Waking and waking in the guarded tomb. . . .

But the armed ocean of peace,
The full-armed ocean is suddenly within us.
Where, where, peace, did you get in?
And the armed ocean of quiet,
The full armed ocean, stands within us:
Where, from what wells, hid in the middle of our essence,
You silences, did you come pouring in?

But all our thoughts lie still, and in this shipwreck
We'll learn the theory of prayer:
"How many hate their own safe death,
Their cell, their submarine!"
"How many hate Your Cross, Your Key, the only one
To beat that last invincible door
That will surprise us, Peace, with Your invasion
And let us in those soundless fathoms where You dwell."   *1947*

SENESCENTE MUNDO

Senescente mundo, when the hot globe
Shrivels and cracks
And uninhibited atoms resolve
Earth and water, fruit and flower, body and animal soul,
All the blue stars come tumbling down.
Beauty and ugliness and love and hate
Wisdom and politics are all alike undone.

Toward that fiery day we run like crabs
With our bad-tempered armor on.
"With blood and carpets, oranges and ashes,
Rubber and limes and bones,"
(So sing the children on the Avenue)
"With cardboard and dirty water and a few flames for the
     Peacelover's ghost,
We know where the dead bodies are
Studying the ceiling from the floors of their homes,
With smoke and roses, slate and wire
And crushed fruit and much fire."

Yet in the middle of this murderous season
Great Christ, my fingers touch Thy wheat

And hold Thee hidden in the compass of Thy paper sun.
There is no war will not obey this cup of Blood,
This wine in which I sink Thy words, in the anonymous dawn!
I hear a Sovereign talking in my arteries
Reversing, with His Promises, all things
That now go on with fire and thunder.
His Truth is greater than disaster.
His Peace imposes silence on the evidence against us.

And though the world, at last, has swallowed her own
    solemn laughter
And has condemned herself to hell:
Suppose a whole new universe, a great clean Kingdom
Were to rise up like an Atlantis in the East,
Surprise this earth, this cinder, with new holiness!

Here in my hands I hold that secret Easter.
Tomorrow, this will be my Mass's answer,
Because of my companions whom the wilderness has eaten,
Crying like Jonas in the belly of our whale.   *1949*

EARLY MASS

(ST. JOSEPH INFIRMARY—LOUISVILLE)

There is a Bread which You and I propose.
It is Your truth. And more: it is ourselves.
There was a wickedness whose end is blessing.
Come, people, to the Cross and Wedding!

His are the mysteries which I expound
And mine the children whom His stars befriend.
Our Christ has cleanly built His sacred town.

What do the windows of His city say?
His innocence is written on your sky!
Because we think His Latin we are part of one another,
Together when I am away.

Come to the ark and stone
Come to the Holies where His work is done,
Dear hasty doves, transparent in His sun!

Gather us God in honeycombs,
My Israel, in the Ohio valley!
For brightness falls upon our dark.

Death owns a wasted kingdom.
Bless and restore the blind, straighten the broken limb.
These mended stones shall build Jerusalem.

Come to the golden fence with folded hands
And see your Bird, kneel to your white Beloved.
Here is your Father at my finger's end!

The clouds are torn. Summon the winds of fall.
On street and water, track and river, shine, November!
Open the doors and own the avenue
For see: we are the makers of a risen world, the brothers of a new
Brown universe whose liturgy
Sweetly consumes my bones.   *1957*

HAGIA SOPHIA

I. *Dawn. The Hour of Lauds.*

There is in all visible things an invisible fecundity, a dimmed light, a meek namelessness, a hidden wholeness. This mysterious Unity and Integrity is Wisdom, the Mother of all, *Natura naturans.* There is in all things an inexhaustible sweetness and purity, a silence that is a fount of action and joy. It rises up in wordless gentleness and flows out to me from the unseen roots of all created being, welcoming me tenderly, saluting me with indescribable humility. This is at once my own being, my own nature, and the Gift of my Creator's Thought and Art within me, speaking as Hagia Sophia, speaking as my sister, Wisdom.

I am awakened, I am born again at the voice of this my Sister, sent to me from the depths of the divine fecundity.

Let us suppose I am a man lying asleep in a hospital. I am indeed this man lying asleep. It is July the second, the Feast of Our Lady's Visitation. A Feast of Wisdom.

At five-thirty in the morning I am dreaming in a very quiet room when a soft voice awakens me from my dream. I am like all mankind awakening from all the dreams that ever were dreamed in all the nights of the world. It is like the One Christ awakening in all the separate selves that ever were separate and isolated and alone in all the lands of the earth. It is like all minds coming back together into awareness from all distractions, cross-purposes and confusions, into unity of love. It is like the first morning of the world (when Adam, at the sweet voice of Wisdom awoke from nonentity and knew her), and like the Last Morning of the world when all the fragments of Adam will return from death at the voice of Hagia Sophia, and will know where they stand.

Such is the awakening of one man, one morning, at the voice of a nurse in the hospital. Awakening out of languor and darkness, out of helplessness, out of sleep, newly confronting reality and finding it to be gentleness.

It is like being awakened by Eve. It is like being awakened by the Blessed Virgin. It is like coming forth from primordial nothingness and standing in clarity, in Paradise.

In the cool hand of the nurse there is the touch of all life, the touch of Spirit.

Thus Wisdom cries out to all who will hear *(Sapientia clamitat in plateis)* and she cries out particularly to the little, to the ignorant and the helpless.

Who is more little, who is more poor than the helpless man who lies asleep in his bed without awareness and without defense? Who is more trusting than he who must entrust himself each night to sleep? What is the reward of his trust? Gentleness comes to him when he is most helpless and awakens him, refreshed, beginning to be made whole. Love takes him by the hand, and opens to him the doors of another life, another day.

(But he who has defended himself, fought for himself in sickness, planned for himself, guarded himself, loved himself alone and watched over his own life all night, is killed at last by exhaustion. For him there is no newness. Everything is stale and old.)

When the helpless one awakens strong at the voice of mercy, it is as if Life his Sister, as if the Blessed Virgin, (his own flesh, his own sister), as if Nature made wise by God's Art and Incarnation were to stand over him and invite him with unutterable sweetness to be awake and to live. This is what it means to recognize Hagia Sophia.

II. *Early Morning. The Hour of Prime.*

O blessed, silent one, who speaks everywhere!

We do not hear the soft voice, the gentle voice, the merciful and feminine.

We do not hear mercy, or yielding love, or non-resistance, or non-reprisal. In her there are no reasons and no answers. Yet she is the candor of God's light, the expression of His simplicity.

We do not hear the uncomplaining pardon that bows down the innocent visages of flowers to the dewy earth. We do not see the Child who is prisoner in all the people, and who says nothing. She smiles, for though they have bound her, she cannot be a prisoner. Not that she is strong, or clever, but simply that she does not understand imprisonment.

The helpless one, abandoned to sweet sleep, him the gentle one will awake: Sophia.

All that is sweet in her tenderness will speak to him on all sides in everything, without ceasing, and he will never be the same again. He will have awakened not to conquest and dark pleasure but to the impeccable pure simplicity of One consciousness in all and through all: one Wisdom, one Child, one Meaning, one Sister.

The stars rejoice in their setting, and in the rising of the Sun. The heavenly lights rejoice in the going forth of one man to make a new world in the morning, because he has come out of the confused primordial dark night into consciousness. He has expressed the clear silence of Sophia in his own heart. He has become eternal.

III. *High Morning. The Hour of Tierce.*

The Sun burns in the sky like the Face of God, but we do not know his countenance as terrible. His light is diffused in the air and the light of God is diffused by Hagia Sophia.

We do not see the Blinding One in black emptiness. He speaks to us gently in ten thousand things, in which His light is one fulness and one Wisdom.

Thus He shines not on them but from within them. Such is the loving-kindness of Wisdom.

All the perfections of created things are also in God; and therefore He is at once Father and Mother. As Father He stands in solitary might surrounded by darkness. As Mother His shining is diffused, embracing all His creatures with merciful tenderness and light. The Diffuse Shining of God is Hagia Sophia. We call her His "glory." In Sophia His power is experienced only as mercy and as love.

(When the recluses of fourteenth-century England heard their Church Bells and looked out upon the wolds and fens under a kind sky, they spoke in their hearts to "Jesus our Mother." It was Sophia that had awakened in their childlike hearts.)

Perhaps in a certain very primitive aspect Sophia is the unknown, the dark, the nameless Ousia. Perhaps she is even the Divine Nature, One in Father, Son and Holy Ghost. And perhaps she is in infinite light unmanifest, not even waiting to be known as Light. This I do not know. Out of the silence Light is spoken. We do not hear it or see it until it is spoken.

In the Nameless Beginning, without Beginning, was the Light. We have not seen this Beginning. I do not know where she is, in this Beginning. I do not speak of her as a Beginning, but as a manifestation.

Now the Wisdom of God, Sophia, comes forth, reaching from "end to end mightily." She wills to be also the unseen pivot of all nature, the center and significance of all the light that is *in* all and *for* all. That which is poorest and humblest, that which is most hidden in all things is nevertheless most obvious in them, and quite manifest, for it is their own self that stands before us, naked and without care.

Sophia, the feminine child, is playing in the world, obvious and unseen, playing at all times before the Creator. Her delights are to be with the children of men. She is their sister. The core of life that exists in all things is tenderness, mercy, virginity, the Light, the Life considered as passive, as received, as given, as taken, as inexhaustibly renewed by the Gift of God. Sophia is Gift, is Spirit, *Donum Dei.* She is God-given and God Himself as Gift. God as all, and God reduced to Nothing: inexhaustible nothingness. *Exinanivit semetipsum.* Humility as the source of unfailing light.

Hagia Sophia in all things is the Divine Life reflected in them, considered as a spontaneous participation, as their invitation to the Wedding Feast.

Sophia is God's sharing of Himself with creatures. His outpouring, and the Love by which He is given, and known, held and loved.

She is in all things like the air receiving the sunlight. In her they prosper. In her they glorify God. In her they rejoice to reflect Him. In her they are united with him. She is the union between them. She is the Love that unites them. She is life as communion, life as thanksgiving, life as praise, life as festival, life as glory.

Because she receives perfectly there is in her no stain. She is love without blemish, and gratitude without self-complacency. All things praise her by being themselves and by sharing in the Wedding Feast. She is the Bride and the Feast and the Wedding.

The feminine principle in the world is the inexhaustible source of creative realizations of the Father's glory. She is His manifestation in radiant splendor! But she remains unseen, glimpsed only by a few. Sometimes there are none who know her at all.

Sophia is the mercy of God in us. She is the tenderness with which the infinitely mysterious power of pardon turns the darkness of our sins into the light of grace. She is the inexhaustible fountain of kindness, and would almost seem to be, in herself, all mercy. So she does in us a greater work than that of Creation: the work of new being in grace, the work of pardon, the work of transformation from brightness to brightness *tamquam a Domini Spiritu.* She is in us the yielding and tender counterpart of the power, justice and creative dynamism of the Father.

IV. *Sunset. The Hour of Compline. Salve Regina.*

Now the Blessed Virgin Mary is the one created being who enacts and shows forth in her life all that is hidden in Sophia. Because of this she can be said to be a personal manifestation of Sophia, Who in God is *Ousia* rather than Person.

Natura in Mary becomes pure Mother. In her, *Natura* is as she was from the origin from her divine birth. In Mary *Natura* is all wise and is manifested as an all-prudent, all-loving, all-pure person: not a Creator, and not a Redeemer, but perfect Creature, perfectly Redeemed, the fruit of all God's great power, the perfect expression of wisdom in mercy.

It is she, it is Mary, Sophia, who in sadness and joy, with the full awareness of what she is doing, sets upon the Second Person, the

Logos, a crown which is His Human Nature. Thus her consent opens the door of created nature, of time, of history, to the Word of God.

God enters into His creation. Through her wise answer, through her obedient understanding, through the sweet yielding consent of Sophia, God enters without publicity into the city of rapacious men.

She crowns Him not with what is glorious, but with what is greater than glory: the one thing greater than glory is weakness, nothingness, poverty.

She sends the infinitely Rich and Powerful One forth as poor and helpless, in His mission of inexpressible mercy, to die for us on the Cross.

The shadows fall. The stars appear. The birds begin to sleep. Night embraces the silent half of the earth. A vagrant, a destitute wanderer with dusty feet, finds his way down a new road. A homeless God, lost in the night, without papers, without identification, without even a number, a frail expendable exile lies down in desolation under the sweet stars of the world and entrusts Himself to sleep.

1962

THE NIGHT OF DESTINY

In my ending is my meaning
Says the season.

No clock:
Only the heart's blood
Only the word.

O lamp
Weak friend
In the knowing night!

O tongue of flame
Under the heart
Speak softly:
For love is black
Says the season.

The red and sable letters
On the solemn page
Fill the small circle of seeing.

Long dark—
And the weak life
Of oil.

Who holds the homeless light secure
In the deep heart's room?

Midnight!
Kissed with flame!
See! See!
My love is darkness!

Only in the Void
Are all ways one:

Only in the night
Are all the lost
Found.

In my ending is my meaning.   *1977*

[UNTITLED]

Five breaths pray in me: sun moon
Rain wind and fire
Five seated Buddhas reign in the breaths
Five illusions
One universe:
The white breath, yellow breath,
Green breath, blue breath,
Red fire breath, Amitabha
Knowledge and Desire
And the quiescence
Of Knowledge and Desire.   *1977*

FOUR

SONGS OF CONTEMPLATION

EVENING

Now, in the middle of the limpid evening,
The moon speaks clearly to the hill.
The wheatfields make their simple music,
Praise the quiet sky.

And down the road, the way the stars come home,
The cries of children
Play on the empty air, a mile or more,
And fall on our deserted hearing,
Clear as water.

They say the sky is made of glass,
They say the smiling moon's a bride.
They say they love the orchards and apple trees,
The trees, their innocent sisters, dressed in blossoms,
Still wearing, in the blurring dusk,
White dresses from that morning's first communion.

And, where blue heaven's fading fire last shines
They name the new come planets
With words that flower
On little voices, light as stems of lilies.

And where blue heaven's fading fire last shines,
Reflected in the poplar's ripple,
One little, wakeful bird
Sings like a shower.   *1944*

Song for Our Lady of Cobre

The white girls lift their heads like trees,
The black girls go
Reflected like flamingoes in the street.
The white girls sing as shrill as water,
The black girls talk as quiet as clay.

The white girls open their arms like clouds,
The black girls close their eyes like wings:
Angels bow down like bells,
Angels look up like toys,

Because the heavenly stars
Stand in a ring:
And all the pieces of the mosaic, earth,
Get up and fly away like birds.   *1944*

Two States of Prayer

In wild October when the low hills lie
With open eye
And own the land like lions,

Our prayer is like the thousands in the far, forgotten stadiums,
Building its exultation like a tower of fire,
Until the marvelous woods spring to their feet
And raid the skies with their red-headed shout:

This is the way our hearts take flame
And burn us down, on pyres of prayer, with too much glory.

But when the trees have all torn up their programs,
Scattering the pathos of immense migrations to the open-handed
    winds,
Clouding and saddening the dusky valley,
Sorrow begins to bully the bare bars
Of those forsaken cages
As thought lies slaughtered in the broken doors.

But by the light of our December mornings,
Though words stand frozen in the voice's well
And all the country pumps are dumb,
Look where the landscape, like a white Cistercian,
Puts on the ample winter like a cowl
And so conceals, beneath the drifts as deep as quietude,
The ragged fences and the ravaged field.

The hills lie still, the woods their Sabbath keep.
The farms, half buried in their winter coats
Are warm as sheep.
When was there ever greater than this penitential peace
Outshining all the songs of June with radiant silences?

November analyzed our bankruptcies, but now
His observations lie knee-deep beneath our Christmas mercies,
While folded in the buried seed
The virtual summer lives and sleeps;
And every acre keeps its treasure like a kingly secret.   *1947*

EVENING: ZERO WEATHER

Now the lone world is streaky as a wall of marble
With veins of clear and frozen snow.
There is no bird-song there, no hare's track

No badger working in the russet grass:
All the bare fields are silent as eternity.

And the whole herd is home in the long barn.
The brothers come, with hoods about their faces,
Following their plumes of breath
Lugging the gleaming buckets one by one.

This was a day when shovels would have struck
Full flakes of fire out of the land like rock:
And ground cries out like iron beneath our boots

When all the monks come in with eyes as clean as the cold sky
And axes under their arms,
Still paying out *Ave Marias*
With rosaries between their bleeding fingers.

We shake the chips out of our robes outside the door
And go to hide in cowls as deep as clouds,
Bowing our shoulders in the church's shadow, lean and whipped,
To wait upon your Vespers, Mother of God!

And we have eyes no more for the dark pillars
    or the freezing windows,
Ears for the rumorous cloister or the chimes of time
    above our heads:
For we are sunken in the summer of our adoration,
And plunge, down, down into the fathoms of our secret joy
That swims with indefinable fire.
And we will never see the copper sunset
Linger a moment, like an echo, on the frozen hill
Then suddenly die an hour before the Angelus.

For we have found our Christ, our August
Here in the zero days before Lent—

We are already binding up our sheaves of harvest
Beating the lazy liturgy, going up with exultation
Even on the eve of our Ash Wednesday,
And entering our blazing heaven by the doors of the Assumption!

1947

THE SOWING OF MEANINGS

See the high birds! Is theirs the song
That flies among the wood-light
Wounding the listener with such bright arrows?

Or do they play in wheeling silences
Defining in the perfect sky
The bounds of (here below) our solitude,

Where spring has generated lights of green
To glow in clouds upon the sombre branches?

Ponds full of sky and stillnesses
What heavy summer songs still sleep
Under the tawny rushes at your brim?

More than a season will be born here, nature,
In your world of gravid mirrors!
The quiet air awaits one note,
One light, one ray and it will be the angels' spring:
One flash, one glance upon the shiny pond, and then
Asperges me! sweet wilderness, and lo! we are redeemed!

For, like a grain of fire
Smouldering in the heart of every living essence
God plants His undivided power—

Buries His thought too vast for worlds
In seed and root and blade and flower,

Until, in the amazing shadowlights
Of windy, cloudy April,
Surcharging the religious silence of the spring
Creation finds the pressure of its everlasting secret
Too terrible to bear.

Then every way we look, lo! rocks and trees
Pastures and hills and streams and birds and firmament
And our own souls within us flash, and shower us with light,
While the wild countryside, unknown, unvisited of men,
Bears sheaves of clean, transforming fire.

And then, oh then the written image, schooled in sacrifice,
The deep united threeness printed in our deepest being,
Shot by the brilliant syllable of such an intuition, turns within,
And plants that light far down into the heart of darkness
        and oblivion
And plunges after to discover flame.   *1947*

A PSALM

When psalms surprise me with their music
And antiphons turn to rum
The Spirit sings: the bottom drops out of my soul

And from the center of my cellar, Love, louder than thunder
Opens a heaven of naked air.

New eyes awaken.
I send Love's name into the world with wings

And songs grow up around me like a jungle.
Choirs of all creatures sing the tunes
Your Spirit played in Eden.

Zebras and antelopes and birds of paradise
Shine on the face of the abyss
And I am drunk with the great wilderness
Of the sixth day in Genesis.

But sound is never half so fair
As when that music turns to air
And the universe dies of excellence.

Sun, moon and stars
Fall from their heavenly towers.
Joys walk no longer down the blue world's shore.

Though fires loiter, lights still fly on the air of the gulf,
All fear another wind, another thunder:
Then one more voice
Snuffs all their flares in one gust.

And I go forth with no more wine and no more stars
And no more buds and no more Eden
And no more animals and no more sea:
While God sings by Himself in acres of night
And walls fall down, that guarded Paradise.   *1949*

ELIAS—VARIATIONS ON A THEME

I
Under the blunt pine
In the winter sun
The pathway dies
And the wilds begin.
Here the bird abides
Where the ground is warm
And sings alone.

Listen, Elias,
To the southern wind
Where the grass is brown,
Live beneath this pine
In wind and rain.
Listen to the woods,
Listen to the ground.

O listen, Elias
(Where the bird abides
And sings alone),
The sun grows pale
Where passes One
Who bends no blade, no fern.
Listen to His word.

> *"Where the fields end*
> *Thou shalt be My friend.*
> *Where the bird is gone*
> *Thou shalt be My son."*

How the pine burns
In the furious sun

When the prophets come
To Jerusalem.
(Listen, Elias,
To the covering wing?)
To Jerusalem
Where the knife is drawn.

(Do her children run
To the covering wing?)
Look, look, My son,
At the smashed wood
At the bloody stone.

Where the fields end
And the stars begin
Listen, Elias,
To the winter rain.
For the seed sleeps
By the sleeping stone.
But the seed has life
While the stone has none.

"Where the fields end
Thou shalt be My friend.
Where the bird is gone
Thou shalt be My son."

II
There were supposed to be
Not birds but spirits of flame
Around the old wagon.
("Bring me my chariot")
There were supposed
To be fiery devices,
Grand machines, all flame,

With supernatural wings
Beyond the full creek.
("Bring me my chariot of fire")
All flame, beyond the rotten tree!
Flame? This old wagon
With the wet, smashed wheels
Is better. ("My chariot")
This derelict is better.
("Of fire.") It abides
(Swifter) in the brown ferns
And burns nothing. Bring me ("Of fire")
Better still the old trailer ("My chariot")
With the dead stove in it, and the rain
Comes down the pipe and covers the floor.
Bring me my chariot of rain. Bring me
My old chariot of broken-down rain.
Bring, bring my old fire, my old storm,
My old trailer; faster and faster it stands still,
Faster and faster it stays where it has always been,
Behind the felled oaks, faster, burning nothing.
Broken and perfect, facing south,
Facing the sound of distant guns,
Facing the wall of distance where blue hills
Hide in the fading rain.

Where the woods are cut down the punished
Trailer stands alone and becomes
(Against all the better intentions of the owners)
The House of God
The Gate of Heaven.
("My chariot of fire")

III
The seed, as I have said,
Hides in the frozen sod.
Stones, shaped by rivers they will

Never care about or feel,
Cover the cultivated soil.
The seed, by nature, waits to grow and bear
Fruit. Therefore it is not alone
As stones, or inanimate things are:
That is to say, alone by nature,
Or alone forever.

Where do so many waters come from on an empty hill?
Rain we had despaired of, rain
Which is sent from somewhere else, descended
To fix an exhausted mountain.
Listen to the waters, if possible,
And discern the words "False prophet"
False prophet! "So much better is the water's message,
So much more confident than our own. It is quite sure
You are a false prophet, so 'Go back'
(You have not had the patience of a rock or tree)
Go back into the cities. They want to receive you
Because you are not sent to them. You are a false prophet."

Go back where everyone, in heavy hours,
Is of a different mind, and each is his own burden,
And each mind is its own division
With sickness for diversion and war for
Business reasons. Go where the divided
Cannot stand to be too well. For then they would be held
Responsible for their own misery.

And I have been a man without silence,
A man without patience, with too many
Questions. I have blamed God
Thinking to blame only men
And defend Him Who does not need to be defended.
I have blamed ("defended") Him for Whom the wise stones

(Stones I lately condemned)
Waited in the patient
Creek that is now wet and clean of all ruins.
So now, if I were to return
To my own city (yes my own city), I would be
Neither accepted nor rejected.
For I have no message,
I would be lost together with the others.

IV
Under the blunt pine
I who am not sent
Remain. The pathway dies,
The journey has begun.
Here the bird abides
And sings on top of the forgotten
Storm. The ground is warm.
He sings no particular message.
His hymn has one pattern, no more planned,
No less perfectly planned
And no more arbitrary
Than the pattern in the seed, the salt,
The snow, the cell, the drop of rain.

   (Snow says: I have my own pattern;
   Rain says: no arbitrary plan!
   River says: I go my own way.
   Bird says: I am the same.
   The pine tree says also:
   Not compulsion plants me in my place,
   No, not compulsion!)

The free man is not alone as busy men are
But as birds are. The free man sings
Alone as universes do. Built

Upon his own inscrutable pattern
Clear, unmistakable, not invented by himself alone
Or for himself, but for the universe also.

Nor does he make it his business to be recognized
Or care to have himself found out
As if some special subterfuge were needed
To get himself known for who he is.

The free man does not float
On the tides of his own expedition
Nor is he sent on ventures as busy men are,
Bound to an inexorable result:
But like the birds or lilies
He seeks first the Kingdom, without care.
Nor need the free man remember
Any street or city, or keep campaigns
In his head, or countries for that matter
Or any other economy.

        Under the blunt pine
Elias becomes his own geography
(Supposing geography to be necessary at all),
Elias becomes his own wild bird, with God in the center,
His own wide field which nobody owns,
His own pattern, surrounding the Spirit
By which he is himself surrounded:

For the free man's road has neither beginning nor end.   *1957*

IN SILENCE

Be still
Listen to the stones of the wall.
Be silent, they try
To speak your

Name.
Listen
To the living walls.
Who are you?
Who
Are you? Whose
Silence are you?

Who (be quiet)
Are you (as these stones
Are quiet). Do not
Think of what you are
Still less of
What you may one day be.
Rather
Be what you are (but who?) be
The unthinkable one
You do not know.

O be still, while
You are still alive,
And all things live around you
Speaking (I do not hear)
To your own being,
Speaking by the Unknown
That is in you and in themselves.

"I will try, like them
To be my own silence:
And this is difficult. The whole
World is secretly on fire. The stones
Burn, even the stones
They burn me. How can a man be still or
Listen to all things burning? How can he dare
To sit with them when
All their silence
Is on fire?"   *1957*

STRANGER

When no one listens
To the quiet trees
When no one notices
The sun in the pool

Where no one feels
The first drop of rain
Or sees the last star

Or hails the first morning
Of a giant world
Where peace begins
And rages end:

One bird sits still
Watching the work of God:
One turning leaf,
Two falling blossoms,
Ten circles upon the pond.

One cloud upon the hillside,
Two shadows in the valley
And the light strikes home.
Now dawn commands the capture
Of the tallest fortune,
The surrender
Of no less marvelous prize!

Closer and clearer
Than any wordy master,
Thou inward Stranger
Whom I have never seen,

Deeper and cleaner
Than the clamorous ocean,
Seize up my silence
Hold me in Thy Hand!

Now act is waste
And suffering undone
Laws become prodigals
Limits are torn down
For envy has no property
And passion is none.

Look, the vast Light stands still
Our cleanest Light is One!   *1957*

GRACE'S HOUSE

On the summit: it stands on a fair summit
Prepared by winds: and solid smoke

Rolls from the chimney like a snow cloud.
Grace's house is secure.

No blade of grass is not counted,
No blade of grass forgotten on this hill.
Twelve flowers make a token garden.
There is no path to the summit—
No path drawn
To Grace's house.

All the curtains are arranged
Not for hiding but for seeing out.
In one window someone looks out and winks.
Two gnarled short
Fortified trees have knotholes
From which animals look out.
From behind a corner of Grace's house
Another creature peeks out.

Important: hidden in the foreground
Most carefully drawn
The dog smiles, his foreleg curled, his eye like an aster.
Nose and collar are made with great attention:
This dog is loved by Grace!

And there: the world!
Mailbox number 5
Is full of Valentines for Grace.
There is a name on the box, name of a family
Not yet ready to be written in language.

A spangled arrow there
Points from our Coney Island
To her green sun-hill.

Between our world and hers
Runs a sweet river:
(No, it is not the road,
It is the uncrossed crystal
Water between our ignorance and her truth.)

O paradise, O child's world!
Where all the grass lives
And all the animals are aware!
The huge sun, bigger than the house
Stands and streams with life in the east
While in the west a thunder cloud
Moves away forever.

No blade of grass is not blessed
On this archetypal, cosmic hill,
This womb of mysteries.

I must not omit to mention a rabbit
And two birds, bathing in the stream
Which is no road, because

Alas, there is no road to Grace's house!   *1963*

SONG FOR NOBODY

A yellow flower
(Light and spirit)
Sings by itself
For nobody.

A golden spirit
(Light and emptiness)

Sings without a word
By itself.

Let no one touch this gentle sun
In whose dark eye
Someone is awake.

(No light, no gold, no name, no color
And no thought:
O, wide awake!)

A golden heaven
Sings by itself
A song to nobody.   *1963*

SONG: IF YOU SEEK . . .

If you seek a heavenly light
I, Solitude, am your professor!

I go before you into emptiness,
Raise strange suns for your new mornings,
Opening the windows
Of your innermost apartment.

When I, loneliness, give my special signal
Follow my silence, follow where I beckon!
Fear not, little beast, little spirit
(Thou word and animal)
I, Solitude, am angel
And have prayed in your name.

Look at the empty, wealthy night
The pilgrim moon!
I am the appointed hour,
The "now" that cuts
Time like a blade.

I am the unexpected flash
Beyond "yes," beyond "no,"
The forerunner of the Word of God.

Follow my ways and I will lead you
To golden-haired suns,
Logos and music, blameless joys,
Innocent of questions
And beyond answers:
For I, Solitude, am thine own self:
I, Nothingness, am thy All.
I, Silence, am thy Amen!   *1963*

O Sweet Irrational Worship

Wind and a bobwhite
And the afternoon sun.

By ceasing to question the sun
I have become light,

Bird and wind.

My leaves sing.

I am earth, earth

All these lighted things
Grow from my heart.

A tall, spare pine
Stands like the initial of my first
Name when I had one.

When I had a spirit,
When I was on fire
When this valley was
Made out of fresh air
You spoke my name
In naming Your silence:
O sweet, irrational worship!

I am earth, earth
My heart's love
Bursts with hay and flowers.
I am a lake of blue air
In which my own appointed place
Field and valley
Stand reflected.

I am earth, earth

Out of my grass heart
Rises the bobwhite.

Out of my nameless weeds
His foolish worship.   *1963*

NIGHT-FLOWERING CACTUS

I know my time, which is obscure, silent and brief
For I am present without warning one night only.

When sun rises on the brass valleys I become serpent.

Though I show my true self only in the dark and to no man
(For I appear by day as serpent)
I belong neither to night nor day.
Sun and city never see my deep white bell
Or know my timeless moment of void:
There is no reply to my munificence.

When I come I lift my sudden Eucharist
Out of the earth's unfathomable joy
Clean and total I obey the world's body
I am intricate and whole, not art but wrought passion
Excellent deep pleasure of essential waters
Holiness of form and mineral mirth:

I am the extreme purity of virginal thirst.

I neither show my truth nor conceal it
My innocence is descried dimly
Only by divine gift
As a white cavern without explanation.

He who sees my purity
Dares not speak of it.
When I open once for all my impeccable bell
No one questions my silence:
The all-knowing bird of night flies out of my mouth.

Have you seen it? Then though my mirth has quickly ended
You live forever in its echo:
You will never be the same again.   *1963*

LOVE WINTER WHEN THE PLANT SAYS NOTHING

O little forests, meekly
Touch the snow with low branches!
O covered stones
Hide the house of growth!

Secret
Vegetal words,
Unlettered water,
Daily zero.

Pray undistracted
Curled tree
Carved in steel—
Buried zenith!

Fire, turn inward
To your weak fort,
To a burly infant spot,
A house of nothing.

O peace, bless this mad place:
Silence, love this growth.

O silence, golden zero
Unsetting sun

Love winter when the plant says nothing.   *1963*

SONG: CONTEMPLATION

O land alive with miracles!
O clad in streams,
Countering the silver summer's pleasant arrows
And beating them with the kind armor
Of your enkindled water-vesture,

Lift your blue trees into the early sun!

O country wild with talent
Is there an hour in you that does not rouse our mind with songs?
The boughs that bend in the weak wind
Open us momentary windows, here and there,
Into those deep and purple galleries,
Disclosing us the birds your genius;

And yet the earth is loud
With more than this their timid vaudeville.

O brilliant wood!
Yours is the voice of a new world;
And all the hills burn with such blinding art

That Christ and angels walk among us, everywhere.
These are their ways, their fiery footsteps,
That flash and vanish, smile and pass;
—By those bright passengers our groves are all inspired.
Lo, we have seen you, we have seized you, wonder,
Caught you, half held you in the larch and lighted birch:
But in that capture you have sailed us half-mile-high into the air
To taste the silences of the inimitable hawk:

Nor do we swing upon the wind
To scan the flattened barns as brown as blood

Growing into the surface of the wounded earth,
Or learn the white roads, livid as a whipcut scar.
For suddenly we have forgotten your geography,
Old nature, and your map of prey,
And know no more the low world scourged with travelling.

The genuine steps, the obvious degrees
The measured cart-ways and the fields we trod all day
And the tunes of the clattering shops,
Even the songs that crowned the highest hill
Find us no longer beggars for their petty coin.
We've left the stations of the mendicants
And the ways of the workaday saints.

But in the dazzled, high and unelectric air
Seized in the talons of the terrible Dove,
The huge, unwounding Spirit,
We suddenly escape the drag of earth
Fly from the dizzy paw of gravity
And swimming in the wind that lies beyond the track
Of thought and genius and of desire,

Trample the white, appalling stratosphere.   *1947*

THE JOY OF FISHES

Chuang Tzu and Hui Tzu
Were crossing Hao river
By the dam.

Chuang said:
"See how free

The fishes leap and dart:
That is their happiness."

Hui replied:
"Since you are not a fish
How do you know
What makes fishes happy?"

Chuang said:
"Since you are not I
How can you possibly know
That I do not know
What makes fishes happy?"

Hui argued:
"If I, not being you,
Cannot know what you know
It follows that you
Not being a fish
Cannot know what they know."

Chuang said:
"Wait a minute!
Let us get back
To the original question.
What you asked me was
'How do you know
What makes fishes happy?'
From the terms of your question
You evidently know I know
What makes fishes happy.

"I know the joy of fishes
In the river
Through my own joy, as I go walking
Along the same river."   *1977*

FIVE

HISTORY'S VOICES: PAST AND PRESENT

DIRGE FOR THE WORLD JOYCE DIED IN

Now ravel up the roots of workman oak trees
And rack apart the knotted limbs of earth:
Ravish the kingdoms of the breeding sun
And scan their ruins for a devil's birth.

Rescue the usurers from the living sea:
Their dead love runs like life, in copper wire.
Their nervousness draws polar fire of metal
To blast the harvest of our prettiest year.

The doctors in their disinfected city
Count the course their shining zodiacs go,
Nor listen to the worms' red work devour them
Curled where some tooth is planted in the jaw.

Suffer no drug to slack his idiot eyestring
Receiving, dumb to prayer, the ascetic blade
Sent to stab out and blind that volunteer:
Proud spy in the cursing kingdom of the dead!   *1940–42 {1971}*

IN MEMORY OF THE SPANISH POET FEDERICO GARCÍA LORCA

Where the white bridge rears up its stamping arches
Proud as a colt across the clatter of the shallow river,
The sharp guitars
Have never forgotten your name.

Only the swordspeech of the cruel strings
Can pierce the minds of those who remain,

Sitting in the eyeless ruins of the houses,
The shelter of the broken wall.

A woman has begun to sing:
O music the color of olives!

Her eyes are darker than the deep cathedrals;
Her words come dressed as mourners,
In the gate of her shadowy voice,
Each with a meaning like a sheaf of seven blades!

The spires and high Giraldas, still as nails
Nailed in the four cross roads,
Watch where the song becomes the color of carnations,
And flowers like wounds in the white dust of Spain.

(Under what crossless Calvary lie your lost bones, García Lorca?
What white Sierra hid your murder in a rocky valley?)

In the four quarters of the world, the wind is still,
And wonders at the swordplay of the fierce guitar:
The voice has turned to iron in the naked air,
More loud and more despairing than a ruined tower.

(Under what crossless Calvary lie your lost bones, García Lorca?
What white Sierra hid your murder in a rocky valley?)

1944

AN ELEGY FOR ERNEST HEMINGWAY

Now for the first time on the night of your death your name is
mentioned in convents, *ne cadas in obscurum.*

Now with a true bell your story becomes final. Now men in monasteries, men of requiems, familiar with the dead, include you in their offices.

You stand anonymous among thousands, waiting in the dark at great stations on the edge of countries known to prayer alone, where fires are not merciless, we hope, and not without end.

You pass briefly through our midst. Your books and writings have not been consulted. Our prayers are *pro defuncto N.*

Yet some look up, as though among a crowd of prisoners or displaced persons, they recognized a friend once known in a far country. For these the sun also rose after a forgotten war upon an idiom you made great. They have not forgotten you. In their silence you are still famous, no ritual shade.

How slowly this bell tolls in a monastery tower for a whole age, and for the quick death of an unready dynasty, and for that brave illusion: the adventurous self!

For with one shot the whole hunt is ended!   *1963*

ELEGY FOR JAMES THURBER

Thurber, they have come, the secret bearers,
At the right time, though fools seem to have won.
Business and generals survive you
At least for one brief day.

Humor is now totally abolished.
The great dogs of nineteen sixty-one
Are nothing to laugh at.

Leave us, good friend. Leave our awful celebration
With pity and relief.
You are not called to solemnize with us
Our final madness.

You have not been invited to hear
The last words of everybody.   *1963*

RILKE'S EPITAPH

"Rose, O pure
Contradiction
Longing to be nobody's
Sleep under so many
Lids."

Pierced by an innocent
Rose, (O pure
Contradiction)
Nobody's lids
And everybody's sleep

Death (Nothing but distance
And unreason)
You accept it,
You pluck it.

Music (O pure
Contradiction)
Everybody's
Vision.   *1977*

MESSAGE TO BE INSCRIBED ON MARK VAN DOREN'S HAMILTON MEDAL

You think we don't have messages in Kentucky? Here is one I got
    by hounds, on the day of a blizzard.

Hounds, hounds, with lolling heads of snow! See them signal:

"Mark's one doorway has opened to the Hamilton medal, a huge
    fabulous piece of gold given away each year for letters."

"Great gold," I cry, "an up-country treat!"

"Country nothing" frown the two efficients, "Mark is a metropolitan
    winner. He is feasted by mayors in city halls, for personal
    eminence."

"Yes" I concur "his eminence may be great, but greater is his
    friendship. For eminence let him be paved all over with gold
    medals. For friendship let him receive alphabets and inscrip-
    tions from friends on the sea, in the air, and in monasteries."

"Let lenten monks meditate upon Mark and the meats of the
    banquet."

"Bring me a piece of coal and a strip of birch bark and I will praise
    Mark's doorway to joy in the Alphabet Medal."

"I will praise Mark all day long for the twenty-six medals of his
    alphabet."

"Of all the great writers I know Mark is the only one with that
    kind of alphabet."   *1977*

Two British Airmen

(BURIED WITH CEREMONY IN THE TEUTOBURG FOREST)

Long buried, ancient men-at-arms
Beneath the beechtrees and the farms
Sleep, and syntax locks their glory
In the old pages of a story.

"We knew that battle when it was
A curious clause in Tacitus,
But were not able to construe
Our graves were in this forest too;
And, buried, never thought to have found
Such strange companions, underground."

"—Bring his flag, and wrap, and lay him
Under a cross that shows no name,
And, in the same ground make his grave
As those long-lost Romans have.
Let him a speechless exile be
From England and his century,
Nor question these old strangers, here,
Inquisitive, around his bier."

Lower, and let the bugle's noise
Supersede the Parson's voice
Who values at too cheap a rate
These men as "servants of their state."
Lower, and let the bombers' noise
Supersede the deacon's voice:
None but perfunctory prayers were said
For the unquiet spirits of these dead.   *1940–42 {1971}*

ORIGINAL CHILD BOMB

POINTS FOR MEDITATION TO BE SCRATCHED ON THE WALLS OF A CAVE

1: In the year 1945 an Original Child was born. The name Original Child was given to it by the Japanese people, who recognized that it was the first of its kind.

2: On April 12th, 1945, Mr. Harry Truman became the President of the United States, which was then fighting the second world war. Mr. Truman was a vice president who became president by accident when his predecessor died of a cerebral hemorrhage. He did not know as much about the war as the president before him did. He knew a lot less about the war than many people did.

About one hour after Mr. Truman became president, his aides told him about a new bomb which was being developed by atomic scientists. They called it the "atomic bomb." They said scientists had been working on it for six years and that it had so far cost two billion dollars. They added that its power was equal to that of twenty thousand tons of TNT. A single bomb could destroy a city. One of those present added, in a reverent tone, that the new explosive might eventually destroy the whole world.

But Admiral Leahy told the President the bomb would never work.

3: President Truman formed a committee of men to tell him if this bomb would work, and if so, what he should do with it. Some members of this committee felt that the bomb would jeopardize the future of civilization. They were against its use. Others wanted it to be used in demonstration on a forest of cryptomeria trees, but not against a civil or military target. Many atomic scientists warned that the use of atomic power in war would be difficult and even impossible to control. The danger would be very great. Finally, there were others who believed that if the bomb were used just once or twice, on one or two Japanese cities, there would be no more war. They believed the new bomb would produce eternal peace.

4: In June 1945 the Japanese government was taking steps to negotiate for peace. On one hand the Japanese ambassador tried to interest the Russian government in acting as a go-between with the United States. On the other hand, an unofficial approach was made secretly through Mr. Allen Dulles in Switzerland. The Russians said they were not interested and that they would not negotiate. Nothing was done about the other proposal which was not official. The Japanese High Command was not in favor of asking for peace, but wanted to continue the war, even if the Japanese mainland were invaded. The generals believed that the war should continue until everybody was dead. The Japanese generals were professional soldiers.

5: In the same month of June, the President's committee decided that the new bomb should be dropped on a Japanese city. This would be a demonstration of the bomb on a civil and military target. As "demonstration" it would be a kind of a "show." "Civilians" all over the world love a good "show." The "destructive" aspect of the bomb would be "military."

6: The same committee also asked if America's friendly ally, the Soviet Union, should be informed of the atomic bomb. Someone suggested that this information would make the Soviet Union even more friendly than it was already. But all finally agreed that the Soviet Union was now friendly enough.

7: There was discussion about which city should be selected as the first target. Some wanted it to be Kyoto, an ancient capital of Japan and a center of the Buddhist religion. Others said no, this would cause bitterness. As a result of a chance conversation, Mr. Stimson, the Secretary of War, had recently read up on the history and beauties of Kyoto. He insisted that this city should be left untouched. Some wanted Tokyo to be the first target, but others argued that Tokyo had already been practically destroyed by fire raids and could no longer be considered a "target." So it was decided Hiroshima was the most opportune target, as it had not yet been bombed at all. Lucky Hiroshima! What others had experienced over a period of four years would happen to Hiroshima in a single day! Much time would be saved, and "time is money!"

8: When they bombed Hiroshima they would put the following out of business: The Ube Nitrogen Fertilizer Company; the Ube Soda Company; the Nippon Motor Oil Company; the Sumitoma Chemical Company; the Sumitoma Aluminum Company; and most of the inhabitants.

9: At this time some atomic scientists protested again, warning that the use of the bomb in war would tend to make the United States unpopular. But the President's committee was by now fully convinced that the bomb had to be used. Its use would arouse the attention of the Japanese military class and give them food for thought.

10: Admiral Leahy renewed his declaration that the bomb would not explode.

11: On the 4th of July, when the United States in displays of fireworks celebrates its independence from British rule, the British and Americans agreed together that the bomb ought to be used against Japan.

12: On July 7th the Emperor of Japan pleaded with the Soviet Government to act as mediator for peace between Japan and the Allies. Molotov said the question would be "studied." In order to facilitate this "study" Soviet troops in Siberia prepared to attack the Japanese. The Allies had, in any case, been urging Russia to join the war against Japan. However, now that the atomic bomb was nearly ready, some thought it would be better if the Russians took a rest.

13: The time was coming for the new bomb to be tested, in the New Mexico desert. A name was chosen to designate this secret operation. It was called "Trinity."

14: At 5:30 A.M. on July 16th, 1945, a plutonium bomb was successfully exploded in the desert at Alamogordo, New Mexico. It was suspended from a hundred foot steel tower which evaporated. There was a fireball a mile wide. The great flash could be seen for a radius of 250 miles. A blind woman miles away said she perceived light. There was a cloud of smoke 40,000 feet high. It was shaped like a toadstool.

15: Many who saw the experiment expressed their satisfaction in religious terms. A semi-official report even quoted a religious book—The New Testament, "Lord, I believe, help thou my unbelief." There was an atmosphere of devotion. It was a great act of faith. They believed the explosion was exceptionally powerful.

16: Admiral Leahy, still a "doubting Thomas," said that the bomb would not explode when dropped from a plane over a city. Others may have had "faith," but he had his own variety of "hope."

17: On July 21st a full written report of the explosion reached President Truman at Potsdam. The report was documented by pictures. President Truman read the report and looked at the pictures before starting out for the conference. When he left his mood was jaunty and his step was light.

18: That afternoon Mr. Stimson called on Mr. Churchill, and laid before him a sheet of paper bearing a code message about the successful test. The message read "Babies satisfactorily born." Mr.

Churchill was quick to realize that there was more in this than met the eye. Mr. Stimson satisfied his legitimate curiosity.

19: On this same day sixty atomic scientists who knew of the test signed a petition that the bomb should not be used against Japan without a convincing warning and an opportunity to surrender.

At this time the U.S.S. Indianapolis, which had left San Francisco on the 18th, was sailing toward the Island of Tinian, with some U-235 in a lead bucket. The fissionable material was about the size of a softball, but there was enough for one atomic bomb. Instructions were that if the ship sank, the Uranium was to be saved first, before any life. The mechanism of the bomb was on board the U.S.S. Indianapolis, but it was not yet assembled.

20: On July 26th the Potsdam declaration was issued. An ultimatum was given to Japan: "Surrender unconditionally or be destroyed." Nothing was said about the new bomb. But pamphlets dropped all over Japan threatened "an enormous air bombardment" if the army would not surrender. On July 26th the U.S.S. Indianapolis arrived at Tinian and the bomb was delivered.

21: On July 28th, since the Japanese High Command wished to continue the war, the ultimatum was rejected. A censored version of the ultimatum appeared in the Japanese press with the comment that it was "an attempt to drive a wedge between the military and the Japanese people." But the Emperor continued to hope that the Russians, after "studying" his proposal, would help to negotiate a peace. On July 30th Mr. Stimson revised a draft of the announcement that was to be made after the bomb was dropped on the Japanese target. The statement was much better than the original draft.

22: On August 1st the bomb was assembled in an airconditioned hut on Tinian. Those who handled the bomb referred to it as

"Little Boy." Their care for the Original Child was devoted and tender.

23: On August 2nd President Truman was the guest of His Majesty King George VI on board the H.M.S. Renown in Plymouth Harbor. The atomic bomb was praised. Admiral Leahy, who was present, declared that the bomb would not work. His Majesty George VI offered a small wager to the contrary.

24: On August 2nd a special message from the Japanese Foreign Minister was sent to the Japanese Ambassador in Moscow. "It is requested that further efforts be exerted. . . Since the loss of one day may result in a thousand years of regret, it is requested that you immediately have a talk with Molotov." But Molotov did not return from Potsdam until the day the bomb fell.

25: On August 4th the bombing crew on Tinian watched a movie of "Trinity" (the Alamogordo Test). August 5th was a Sunday but there was little time for formal worship. They said a quick prayer that the war might end "very soon." On that day, Col. Tibbetts, who was in command of the B–29 that was to drop the bomb, felt that his bomber ought to have a name. He baptized it Enola Gay, after his mother in Iowa. Col. Tibbetts was a well balanced man, and not sentimental. He did not have a nervous breakdown after the bombing, like some of the other members of the crew.

26: On Sunday afternoon "Little Boy" was brought out in procession and devoutly tucked away in the womb of Enola Gay. That evening few were able to sleep. They were as excited as little boys on Christmas Eve.

27: At 1:37 A.M. August 6th the weather scout plane took off. It was named the Straight Flush, in reference to the mechanical action of a water closet. There was a picture of one, to make this evident.

28: At the last minute before taking off Col. Tibbetts changed the secret radio call sign from "Visitor" to "Dimples." The Bombing Mission would be a kind of flying smile.

29: At 2:45 A.M. Enola Gay got off the ground with difficulty. Over Iwo Jima she met her escort, two more B–29s, one of which was called the Great Artiste. Together they proceeded to Japan.

30: At 6:40 they climbed to 31,000 feet, the bombing altitude. The sky was clear. It was a perfect morning.

31: At 8:09 they reached Hiroshima and started the bomb run. The city was full of sun. The fliers could see the green grass in the gardens. No fighters rose up to meet them. There was no flak. No one in the city bothered to take cover.

32: The bomb exploded within 100 feet of the aiming point. The fireball was 18,000 feet across. The temperature at the center of the fireball was 100,000,000 degrees. The people who were near the center became nothing. The whole city was blown to bits and the ruins all caught fire instantly everywhere, burning briskly. 70,000 people were killed right away or died within a few hours. Those who did not die at once suffered great pain. Few of them were soldiers.

33: The men in the plane perceived that the raid had been successful, but they thought of the people in the city and they were not perfectly happy. Some felt they had done wrong. But in any case they had obeyed orders. "It was war."

34: Over the radio went the code message that the bomb had been successful: "Visible effects greater than Trinity . . . Proceeding to Papacy." Papacy was the code name for Tinian.

35: It took a little while for the rest of Japan to find out what had happened to Hiroshima. Papers were forbidden to publish any news of the new bomb. A four line item said that Hiroshima had been hit by incendiary bombs and added: "It seems that some damage was caused to the city and its vicinity."

36: Then the military governor of the Prefecture of Hiroshima issued a proclamation full of martial spirit. To all the people without hands, without feet, with their faces falling off, with their intestines hanging out, with their whole bodies full of radiation, he declared: "We must not rest a single day in our war effort . . . We must bear in mind that the annihilation of the stubborn enemy is our road to revenge." He was a professional soldier.

37: On August 8th Molotov finally summoned the Japanese Ambassador. At last neutral Russia would give an answer to the Emperor's inquiry. Molotov said coldly that the Soviet Union was declaring war on Japan.

38: On August 9th another bomb was dropped on Nagasaki, though Hiroshima was still burning. On August 11th the Emperor overruled his high command and accepted the peace terms dictated at Potsdam. Yet for three days discussion continued, until on August 14th the surrender was made public and final.

39: Even then the Soviet troops thought they ought to fight in Manchuria "just a little longer." They felt that even though they could not, at this time, be of help in Japan, it would be worth while if they displayed their good will in Manchuria, or even in Korea.

40: As to the Original Child that was now born, President Truman summed up the philosophy of the situation in a few words. "We found the bomb" he said "and we used it."

41: Since that summer many other bombs have been "found." What is going to happen? At the time of writing, after a season of brisk speculation, men seem to be fatigued by the whole question.

1962

PAPER CRANES:

(THE HIBAKUSHA COME TO GETHSEMANI)

How can we tell a paper bird
Is stronger than a hawk
When it has no metal for talons?
It needs no power to kill
Because it is not hungry.

Wilder and wiser than eagles
It ranges round the world
Without enemies
And free of cravings.

The child's hand
Folding these wings
Wins no wars and ends them all.

Thoughts of a child's heart
Without care, without weapons!
So the child's eye
Gives life to what it loves
Kind as the innocent sun
And lovelier than all dragons!   *1977*

CHANT TO BE USED IN PROCESSIONS AROUND A SITE
WITH FURNACES

How we made them sleep and purified them

How we perfectly cleaned up the people and worked a big heater

I was the commander I made improvements and installed a guaranteed system taking account of human weakness I purified and I remained decent

How I commanded

I made cleaning appointments and then I made the travellers sleep and after that I made soap

I was born into a Catholic family but as these people were not going to need a priest I did not become a priest I installed a perfectly good machine it gave satisfaction to many

When trains arrived the soiled passengers received appointments for fun in the bathroom they did not guess

It was a very big bathroom for two thousand people it awaited arrival and they arrived safely

There would be an orchestra of merry widows not all the time much art

If they arrived at all they would be given a greeting card to send home taken care of with good jobs wishing you would come to our joke

Another improvement I made was I built the chambers for two thousand invitations at a time the naked votaries were disinfected with Zyklon B

Children of tender age were always invited by reason of their youth they were unable to work they were marked out for play

They were washed like the others and more than the others

Very frequently women would hide their children in the piles of
    clothing but of course when we came to find them we would
    send the children into the chamber to be bathed

How often I commanded and made improvements and sealed the
    door on top there were flowers the men came with crystals I
    guaranteed the crystal parlor

I guaranteed the chamber and it was sealed you could see through
    portholes

They waited for the shower it was not hot water that came through
    vents though efficient winds gave full satisfaction portholes
    showed this

The satisfied all ran together to the doors awaiting arrival it was
    guaranteed they made ends meet

How I could tell by their cries that love came to a full stop I found
    the ones I had made clean after about a half hour

Jewish male inmates then worked up nice they had rubber boots
    in return for adequate food I could not guess their appetite

Those at the door were taken apart out of a fully stopped love by
    rubber made inmates strategic hair and teeth being used later
    for defense

Then the males removed all clean love rings and made away with
    happy gold

How I commanded and made soap 12 lbs fat 10 quarts water 8 oz
    to a lb of caustic soda but it was hard to find any fat

A big new firm promoted steel forks operating on a cylinder they got the contract and with faultless workmanship delivered very fast goods

"For transporting the customers we suggest using light carts on wheels a drawing is submitted"

"We acknowledge four steady furnaces and an emergency guarantee"

"I am a big new commander operating on a cylinder I elevate the purified materials boil for 2 to 3 hours and then cool"

For putting them into a test fragrance I suggested an express elevator operated by the latest cylinder it was guaranteed

Their love was fully stopped by our perfected ovens but the love rings were salvaged

Thanks to the satisfaction of male inmates operating the heaters without need of compensation our guests were warmed

All the while I had obeyed perfectly

So I was hanged in a commanding position with a full view of the site plant and grounds

You smile at my career but you would do as I did if you knew yourself and dared

In my day we worked hard we saw what we did our self-sacrifice was conscientious and complete our work was faultless and detailed

Do not think yourself better because you burn up friends and enemies with long-range missiles without ever seeing what you have done

1963

EPITAPH FOR A PUBLIC SERVANT

In Memoriam—Adolf Eichmann

"Not out of mercy
Did I launch this transaction"

Relations with father mother brother
Sister most normal
Most desirable
Not out of mercy
A man
With positive ideas
(This transaction)
A Christian
Education
(Not out of mercy)
With private reasons
For not hating Jews

"Not out of mercy did I
Launch this"
Christian education
Without rancor
Without any reason
For hating

"I ENTERED LIFE ON EARTH
IN THE ASPECT OF A HUMAN BEING
AND BELIEVED
IN THE HIGHER MEANING"

Without ill-feeling
Or any reason for
This prize-winning transaction

"I ENTERED LIFE ON EARTH"
To launch a positive idea
"But repentance is for little children"

I entered life on earth
Bearing a resemblance
To man
With this transaction
In my pocket
Relations most normal
Most desirable
Father mother brother sister
In the aspect
Of human beings
One and all without any reason
For ill will or discourtesy
To any Hebrew
Or to Israel
But without
Ideas

"Repentance is
For desirable
Little children"

Without any transaction.

ii

"I NEVER HARBORED ANY ILL FEELING
AGAINST THE JEWS DURING THIS ENTIRE TRANSACTION
I EVEN WALKED THROUGH THE STREETS
WITH A JEWISH FRIEND

HE THOUGHT NOTHING OF IT."

iii

Yet I was saddened at the order
I lost all joy in my
Work

To regain my joy
Without any reason
I joined the Party
I was swallowed by the
Party
Without previous
Decision and entered
Upon my apprenticeship
In Jewish
Affairs.

Saddened at the Order
And the merciless
Affairs
Of my learning
Fast
To forget
I resigned from various
Associations dedicated
To merriment lectures
And Humor refined
Humor!

From then on
Official orders
Were my only language

Repentance is for little children

iv

I lost all joy
In my work
And entered life on earth
In the aspect of a human
Believer.

They were all hostile.

The Leader's success alone
Proved that I should subordinate myself
To such a man
(Relations most normal)
Who was to have his own thoughts in such a matter?
In such a transaction?
Who was I
To judge
The Master?

I lost all joy
I believed in destiny.

I learned to forget
The undesirable Jew.

v

I was born among knives and scissors.

One of the few gifts fate
Bestowed on me is a gift
For truth in so far as it
Depends on myself.

I make it depend
On myself.

Gifted.

They were all hostile.

Repentance is
For little children

Depending on knives and scissors

vi

To grant a mercy death
Institutional care

Not out of mercy
Did I dare

To launch an institution
Or the gifted Leader's
Solution
Not out of mercy
Did I dare

O the carefree relation
The well-run institution
The well-planned
Charitable care

To grant a mercy killing summer
Vacation
To the hero nation
Not out of mercy
Did I dare

I welcomed one and all
To the charity ball
In the charitable foundation
For the chosen nation
I spent my sleepless nights
In care

Who was to have his own thoughts
I granted
To very many
A mercy death
With institutional
Care.

I never asked
For any reward.

vii

At the end
A leaderless life.

No pertinent ordinances
To consult

Not out of mercy
Did I launch this transaction

No pertinent orders
Lolita? "An unwholesome book"

Repentance is for little children

viii

As I entered it
So I left it
LIFE
In the aspect
Of a human
Being

A man with positive
Ideas
With no ill will
Toward any Jew

A man without reason
To hate his fellow citizen
Swallowed up by death
Without previous decision
A Believer

Long live Argentina
Long live Germany
We will meet again
And again
We have been chosen partners
Not out of mercy
Amid knives and scissors
In a positive transaction
Without any reason
For serious concern

WHO THEN SHALL CHERISH HIS OWN THOUGHTS?

Gentlemen Adios
We shall meet again

We shall again be partners
Life is short
Art is long
And we shall meet
Without the slightest
Discourtesy

Repentance is
For little children.   *1977*

A PICTURE OF LEE YING

She wears old clothes she holds a borrowed handkerchief and her
sorrow shows us the papers have bad news again today Lee Ying
only 19 has to return to China

Days on foot with little or no food the last six days on water alone
now she must turn back

Three hundred thousand like her must turn back to China there is
no room say the officials in Hong Kong you must go back where
you came from

Point of no return is the caption but this is meaningless she must
return that is the story

She would not weep if she had reached a point of no return what
she wants is not to return

There is no place for her and no point for thousands like her there
is no point

Their flight from bad news to worse news has caused alarm

Refugees suffer and authorities feel alarm the press does not take
sides

We know all about the sorrow of Lee Ying one glance is enough
we look at something else

She must go back where she came from no more need be said

Whenever the authorities are alarmed everyone must return to
China

We too know all about sorrow we have seen it in the movies

You have our sympathy Miss Lee Ying you must go where we are
sorry for your future

Too bad some people get all the rough breaks the authorities regret

Refugees from China have caused alarm

When the authorities are alarmed what can you do

You can return to China

Their alarm is worse than your sorrow

Please do not look only at the dark side in private life these are
kind men

They are only obeying orders

Over there is Red China where you will remain in future

There also the authorities are alarmed and they too obey orders

Please do not look only at the dark side

All the newspapers in the free world explain why you return their
readers understand how you feel

You have the sympathy of millions

As a tribute to your sorrow we resolve to spend more money on
nuclear weapons there is always a bright side

If this were only a movie a boat would be available have you ever
seen our movies they end happily

You would lean at the rail with "him" the sun would set on China
kiss and fade

You would marry one of the kind authorities

In our movies there is no law higher than love in real life duty is
higher

You would not want the authorities to neglect duty

How do you like the image of the free world sorry you cannot stay

This is the first and last time we will see you in our papers

When you are back home remember us we will be having a good
time   *1963*

AND THE CHILDREN OF BIRMINGHAM

And the children of Birmingham
Walked into the story
Of Grandma's pointed teeth
("Better to love you with")
Reasonable citizens
Rose to exhort them all:
"Return at once to schools of friendship.
Buy in stores of love and law."

(And tales were told
Of man's best friend, the Law.)
And the children of Birmingham
Walked in the shadow
Of Grandma's devil

Smack up against
The singing wall.
Fire and water
Poured over everyone:
"Hymns were extreme,
So there could be no pardon!"

And old Grandma
Began the lesson
Of everybody's skin,
Everybody's fun:
"Liberty may bite
An irresponsible race
Forever singing,"
Grandma said,
"Forever making love:
Look at all the children!"

(And tales were told
Of man's best friend, the Law.)

And the children of Birmingham
Walked into the fury
Of Grandma's hug:
Her friendly cells
("Better to love you with.")
Her friendly officers
And "dooms of love."
Laws had a very long day
And all were weary.

But what the children did that time
Gave their town
A name to be remembered!

(And tales were told
Of man's best friend, the Law.)   *1963*

PICTURE OF A BLACK CHILD WITH A WHITE DOLL

Carole Denise McNair, killed in Birmingham, Sept. 1963

Your dark eyes will never need to understand
Our sadness who see you
Hold that plastic glass-eyed
Merchandise as if our empty-headed race
Worthless full of fury
Twanging and drooling in the southern night
With guns and phantoms
Needed to know love

(Yet how deep the wound and the need
And how far down our hell
Are questions you need not
Answer now)

That senseless platinum head
Of a hot city cupid
Not yet grown to whore's estate
It glories and is dull
Next to your live and lovely shade
Your smile and your person
Yet that silly manufactured head
Would soon kill you if it could think
Others as empty do and will
For no reason
Except for that need
Which you know without malice

And by a better instinct
The need for love.

So without a thought
Of death or fear
Of night
You glow full of dark ripe August
Risen and Christian
Africa purchased
For the one lovable Father alone.

And what was ever darkest and most frail
Was then your treasure-child
So never mind
They found you and made you a winner
Even in most senseless cruelty
Your darkness and childhood
Became fortune yes became
Irreversible luck and halo.   *1977*

APRIL 4TH 1968

                                        For Martin Luther King

On a rainy night
On a rainy night in April
When everybody ran
Said the minister

On a balcony
Of a hotel in Tennessee
"We came at once
Upstairs"

On a night
On a rainy night in April
When the shot was fired
Said the minister

"We came at once upstairs
And found him lying
After the tornado
On the balcony
We came at once upstairs"

On a rainy night
He was our hope
And we found a tornado
Said the minister.

And a well-dressed white man
Said the minister.
Dropped the telescopic storm

And he ran
(The well-dressed minister of death)
He ran
He ran away

And on the balcony
Said the minister
We found
Everybody dying   *1977*

SENECA

When the torch is taken
And the room is dark
The mute wife
Knowing Seneca's ways
Listens to night
To rumors
All around the house
While her wise
Lord promenades
Within his own temple
Master and censor
Overseeing
His own ways
With his philosophical sconce
Policing the streets
Of this secret Rome
While the wife
Silent as a sea
Policing nothing
Waits in darkness
For the Night Bird's
Inscrutable cry.   *1977*

ORIGEN

His sin was to speak first
Among mutes. Learning
Was heresy. A great Abbot
Flung his books in the Nile.

Philosophy destroyed him.
Yet when the smoke of fallen cities
Drifted over the Roman sea
From Gaul to Sicily, Rufinus,
Awake in his Italian room
Lit this mad lighthouse, *beatus*
Ignis amoris, for the whole West.

All who admired him gave him names
Of gems or metals:—"Adamant." Jerome
Said his guts were brass;
But having started with this pretty
Word he changed, another time,
To hatred.
And the Greeks destroyed their jewel
For "frightful blasphemy"
Since he had said hell-fire
Would at last go out,
And all the damned repent.
("Whores, heretics," said Bede,
Otherwise a gentle thinker.
"All the crowd of the wicked,
Even the devil with his regiments
Go free in his detestable opinion.")

To that same hell was Origen then sent
By various pontiffs
To try the truth of his own doctrine.
Yet saints had visions of him
Saying he "did not suffer so much":
He had "erred out of love."
Mechtilde of Magdeburg knew him altogether pardoned
(Though this was still secret
The Curia not having been informed).

As for his heroic mistake—the wild operation
Though brusque, was admitted practical
Fornicationem efficacissime fugiens.

In the end, the medieval West
Would not renounce him. All antagonists,
Bernards and Abelards together, met in this
One madness for the sweet poison
Of compassion in this man
Who thought he heard all beings
From stars to stones, angels to elements, alive
Crying for the Redeemer with a live grief.   *1977*

FALL '66

                    Arturumque etiam sub terris bella moventem.

Green bearded Arthur with his men still blinking from
          underground wars
Comes crawling out of the ivy. They fumble
With their weapons. Gather at the federal table
A party of ancient hoods
Nodding in the blue shadow
Pirates waiting for the new raids.
Infernal smoke
Fills Washington and Camelot
And ashes cut the sight of red-eyed intelligence.

Now Patria sets her stone vision
Toward the computer castles in the vortex;
Is critical of mist;
She alarms the police
And points a solid marble finger

In a general direction:
("There, in the Far East, are the malefactors!")

The granite nation is ugly now
But firm, consoled
By a coat of rhetoric
And soil of pigeons.

Local songs call guards to order.
The earth shakes. Will all the concrete
Stagger and fall?

Or will these armed phantoms
Swim death's ocean and win?

Win what? The earth shakes.
The war is busy in the underground
And hell is ready in the submarines.   *1977*

SIX

ENGAGING THE WORLD

The Philosophers

As I lay sleeping in the park,
Buried in the earth,
Waiting for the Easter rains
To drench me in their mirth
And crown my seedtime with some sap and growth,

Into the tunnels of my ears
Two anaesthetic voices came.
Two mandrakes were discussing life
And Truth and Beauty in the other room.

"Body is truth, truth body. Fat is all
We grow on earth, or all we breed to grow."
Said one mandrake to the other.
Then I heard his brother:
"Beauty is troops, troops beauty. Dead is all
We grow on earth, or all we breed to grow."

As I lay dreaming in the earth,
Enfolded in my future leaves,
My rest was broken by these mandrakes
Bitterly arguing in their frozen graves.   *1940–42 {1971}*

Tower of Babel

THE POLITICAL SPEECH

History is a dialogue between
forward and backward
going inevitably forward
by the misuse of words.

Now the function of the word is:
To designate first the machine,
Then what the machine produces
Then what the machine destroys.
Words show us these things not only in order to mean them
But in order to provoke them
And to incorporate us in their forward movement:
Doing, making, destroy or rather
Being done, being made, being destroyed.
Such is history.

The forgotten principle is that the machine
Should always destroy the maker of the machine
Being more important than the maker
Insofar as man is more important than God.
Words also reflect this principle
Though they are meant to conceal it
From the ones who are too young to know.

Thus words have no essential meaning.
They are means of locomotion
From backward to forward
Along an infinite horizontal plane,
Created by the history which they themselves destroy.
They are the makers of our only reality
The backward-forward working of the web
The movement into the web.   *1940–42 {1971}*

A LETTER TO AMERICA

America, when you were born, and when the plains
Spelled out their miles of praises in the sun
What glory and what history
The rivers seemed to prepare.
We hear them, now, in the Kentucky summer,
While all the locusts drown our forests in their iron prayer:
And we dream of you, beloved, sleeping in your leafy bosom.

How long are we to wake
With eyes that turn to wells of blood
Seeing the hell that gets you from us
With his treacherous embrace!

The bands that raced our flesh
With smiles as raw as scars,
Can kill you, Kansas, with their high-powered thirst.
Have you not heard the vast Missouri sing
To drown them with those billion gallon silences?

But when the day is quieter
Than your primeval cradle
All our green woods fill, once again, with wishful lies:
Maybe the cities, (sing the birds, our travellers)
Maybe the cities have begun to heal,
And stanched their smoky hemorrhage:
Maybe they have begun to mend their cauteries,
Parsing the muteness of so many dead.

Down where the movies grit
Their white electric teeth,
Maybe the glorious children have rebelled
And rinsed their mental slums
In the clean drench of an incalculable grief.

Maybe their penitence has torn the phony sunset
To view their devil dressed in laudanum,
And scotched his crazy spectre,
And learned the liberty of the unfathomable stars,
Within the doors of their confessionals,
Their new, more lasting Lexingtons!

But oh! the flowering cancers of that love
That eats your earth with roots of steel!
No few fast hours can drain your flesh
Of all those seas of candied poison,

Until our long Gregorian cry
Bows down the stars' Samaritan
To rue the pity of so cruel a murder.   *1947*

from CABLES TO THE ACE
OR
FAMILIAR LITURGIES OF MISUNDERSTANDING

For Robert Lax

PROLOGUE

You, Reader, need no prologue. Do you think these Horatian Odes are all about you? Far from the new wine to need a bundle. You are no bundle. Go advertise yourself.
Why not more pictures? Why not more rhythms, melody, etc.? All suitable questions to be answered some other time. The realm of spirit is two doors down the hall. There you can obtain more soul than you are ready to cope with, Buster.
The poet has not announced these mosaics on purpose. Furthermore he has changed his address and his poetics are on vacation.
He is not roaring in the old tunnel.
Go shake hands with the comics if you demand a preface. My attitudes are common and my ironies are no less usual than the bright pages of your favorite magazine. The soaps, the smells, the liquors, the insurance, the third, dull, gin-soaked cheer: what more do you want, Rabble?
Go write your own prologue.
I am the incarnation of everybody and the zones of reassurance.
I am the obstetrician of good fortune. I live in the social cages of joy.
It is morning, afternoon or evening. Begin.
I too have slept here in my stolen Cadillac.
I too have understudied the Paradise swan.

1
Edifying cables can be made musical if played and sung by full-armed societies doomed to an electric war. A heavy imperturbable beat. No indication where to stop. No messages to decode. Cables

are never causes. Noises are never values. With the unending vroom vroom vroom of the guitars we will all learn a new kind of obstinacy, together with massive lessons of irony and refusal. We assist once again at the marriage of heaven and hell.

2

A seer interprets the ministry of the stars, the broken gear of a bird. He tests the quality of stone lights, ashen fruits of a fire's forgotten service. He registers their clarity with each new lurch into suspicion. He does not regret for he does not know. He plots the nativity of the pole star, but it neither sets nor rises. Snow melts on the surface of the young brown river, and there are two lids: the petals of sleep. The sayings of the saints are put away in air-conditioned archives.

3

Decoding the looks of opposites. Writing down their silences. Words replaced by moods. Actions punctuated by the hard fall of imperatives. More and more smoke. Since language has become a medium in which we are totally immersed, there is no longer any need to say anything. The saying says itself all around us. No one need attend. Listening is obsolete. So is silence. Each one travels alone in a small blue capsule of indignation. (Some of the better informed have declared war on language.)

7

ORIGINAL SIN

(A MEMORIAL ANTHEM FOR FATHER'S DAY)

Weep, weep, little day
For the Father of the lame
Experts are looking
For his name

Weep, weep little day
For your Father's bone

All the expeditions
Dig him one.

He went on one leg
Or maybe four
Science (cautious)
Says "Two or more."

Weep weep little day
For his walking and talking
He walked on two syllables
Or maybe none

Weep little history
For the words he offended
One by one
Beating them grievously
With a shin bone.

8

Write a prayer to a computer? But first of all you have to find out
how It thinks. *Does It dig prayer?* More important still, does It dig
me, and father, mother, etc., etc.? How does one begin: "O Thou
great unalarmed and humorless electric sense . . ."? Start out
wrong and you give instant offense. You may find yourself shipped
off to the camps in a freight car. Prayer is a virtue. But don't begin
with the wrong number.

10

Warm sun. Perhaps these yellow wild-flowers have the minds of
little girls. My worship is a blue sky and ten thousand crickets in
the deep wet hay of the field. My vow is the silence under their
song. I admire the woodpecker and the dove in simple mathemat-
ics of flight. Together we study practical norms. The plowed and
planted field is red as a brick in the sun and says: *"Now my turn!"*
Several of us begin to sing.

12

Another sunny birthday. I am tormented by poetry and loss. The summer morning approaches with shy, tentative mandibles. There are perhaps better solutions than to be delicately eaten by an entirely favorable day. But the day is bright with love and with riches for the unconcerned. A black butterfly dances on the blond light of hot cement. My loneliness is nourished by the smell of freshly cut grass, and the distant complaint of a freight train. Nine even strokes of the bell fall like a slowly counted fortune into the far end of my mind while I walk out at the other end of awareness into a very new hot morning in which all the symbols have to be moved. Here is another smiling Jewish New Year and the myths are about to be changed. We will start up brand new religious engines in the multiple temples. Tonight the dark will come alive with fireworks and age will have scored another minor festival.

13

(THE PLANET OVER EASTERN PARKWAY)

In the region of daffodils
And accurate fears
We seek the layout
The scene of claims

We expect 8 A.M.
With cries of racers
"Here is the entrance
To the start"

And the smart pistol
Glints in the eyes
Of an eternal chief
He sees executives
Begin to run
Over fresh cut graves

The whole civic order
Of salads
Blest and green
By order of the town.

Then the machine
With sterling efforts
Keeps in trim
In tune with oil
Though it needs essential grooves
Say the keepers

And you are always turning it off
Says the owner.

So now it is over
The day of executions
Malfeasances are over and done
In all the books of law

And the cart wheel planet
Goes down in the silos of earth
Whose parkways vanish in the steam
Of ocean feeling
Or the houses of oil-men

Go home go home
And get your picture taken
In a bronze western
An ocean of free admissions
To the houses of night
To the sandy electric stars
And the remaining adventures
Of profiteers.

38

Follow the ways of no man, not even your own. The way that is most yours is no way. For where are you? Unborn! Your way therefore is unborn. Yet you travel. You do not become unborn by stopping a journey you have begun: and you cannot be nowhere by issuing a decree: "I am now nowhere!"

50

Give me a cunning dollar that tells me no lie
Better informed
Truth-telling twenties
And fifties that understand

I want to carry
Cracking new money
That knows and loves me
And is my intimate all-looking doctor
Old costly whiteheaded
Family friend
I want my money
To know me like whiskey
I want it to forgive
Past present and future

Make me numb
And advertise
My buzzing feedbacking
Business-making mind

O give me a cunning dollar
That tells the right time
It will make me president and sport
And tell me all the secrets
Of the telephone.

I want to know the new combinations
In my pocket I need to possess
Plato's Mother I want
What knows all the scores
And I want my money
To write me business letters
Early every day.

75

I seek you in the hospital where you work. Will you be a patch of
white moving rapidly across the end of the next hall? I begin again
in every shadow, surrounded by the sound of scandal and the
buzzer calling all doctors to the presence of alarm.

76

After that we'll meet in some Kingdom they forgot and there the
found will play the songs of the sent. Surely a big bird with all the
shades of light will beat against our windows. We will then gladly
consent to the kindness of rays and recover the warm knowledge of
each other we once had under those young trees in another May. (It
is a big bird flies right out of the center of the sun.)

80

Slowly slowly
Comes Christ through the garden
Speaking to the sacred trees
Their branches bear his light
Without harm

Slowly slowly
Comes Christ through the ruins
Seeking the lost disciple
A timid one
Too literate
To believe words
So he hides

Slowly slowly
Christ rises on the cornfields
It is only the harvest moon
The disciple
Turns over in his sleep
And murmurs:
"My regret!"

The disciple will awaken
When he knows history
But slowly slowly
The Lord of History
Weeps into the fire.

82
It rained dark and cold on the Day of St. Theresa of the Heart
For no one yet knew that it was holiday fifteen
It rained like weather in honor of her sacred love
For the notables had built a black stone wall around her heart
And the prelates, mayors, and confessors wanted the doors closed.
The tongue of her heart, they said, must proffer insults to the
      vision.
So they built four walls of cold rain around the vision.
And the rain came down upon the vision in honor of her love.
In the theological cell where she was locked alone with the vision
Her heart was pierced by a thousand needles of fire.
Then the mayors, prelates, and confessors all wept together in
      honor of her love.
They went together in procession to the rainy city walls and
      fortified
Their minds, wrapping them in the folds of the black storm.
Behind them in the invisible town the jails and convents
      overflowed with flame.
In the smallest window of all St. Theresa
Forgotten by these entranced jokers turned her heart into a dove.

The rain ended at that moment.
The dove had flown into the fiery center of the vision.

85

The flash of falling metals. The shower of parts, cameras, guns of experience in the waste heaven of deadly rays. Cataclysm of designs. Out of the meteor sky cascades the efficient rage of our team. Down comes another blazing and dissolute unit melting in mid-air over a fortunate suburb. A perishing computer blazes down into a figure of fire and steam. We live under the rain of stainless leaders. They strike themselves out like matches and fizz for our conjecture in the streets of Taurus. Gone is another technical spy in giant and instant heat. Gone is another tested explorer. Gone is another brilliant intuition of an engineer.

87

I am about to make my home
In the bell's summit
Set my mind a thousand feet high
On the ace of songs
In a mood of needles and random lights
To purify
The quick magnetic sodas of the skin

I will call the deep protectors out of the ground
The givers of wine
The writers of peace and waste
And sundown riddles

The threat of winter gleams in gray-haired windows
And witty mirrors
And fear lies over the sea
But birds fly uncorrected across burnt lands
The surest home is pointless:
We learn by the cables of orioles

I am about to build my nest
In the misdirected and unpaid express
As I walk away from this poem

Hiding the ace of freedoms   *1968*

from THE GEOGRAPHY OF LOGRAIRE

SOUTH

I.
Will a narrow lane
Save Cain?

The Lamb the killer's friend
Skinned in meetings
Has a raw road and it may rain

WE ALL KNOW CAIN MAY BE THE LONGER RUNNER

High stocks buy Betterman's
Sweet Rosy Country Cross
Captain's a wanted Rosicrucian
Traitor to peevish liquor
Kills a brother in the outside lane

LAMB ADMITS TIES TO CAIN

Flashlight umbrella
Casts blood beam
On Daisy Violet Zinnia
Buttercup Rose
Angry under some steps,
Some rain!

Cain and Daisy lock their golden eyes
We all know Cain
But can a Lamb save Cain the raider?

"Maybe he has two manors one for Sundays
One for weeks anger kicked out nigger

Don't come no more white nigger door
Keep out of here"

Go back sore to wait writing
Where happiness beasts will wait behind a store
A bloody sight for sore eyes
"Top fun for D Tremens above the waist"

HOW WOULD YOU LIKE TO LIVE IN THIS PLACE?

It may be two men met Sunday ten
Wearing their whole wheat hats
Saw Satan with a dark knife cut tobacco
When High Green and Corngod stand together
Over Kentucky's corrugated temper
All wet nightlife to Cain and waif

TEN GUNS ARE OUT OF WORK UP ANGER HOLLOW

Try outsmart Saturday's night air
Tight teller sees city split where
Manmade bloodrains light and chemistry wet
Upon blue grass signs the red flower forever

AND KEEP CAIN OUT OF THAT HOLLOW

"I think we owe you an apology mister part time revolver
Mister tallhat individual smell
All sixfoot fires began on Mars landing Friday
When they found the oilwell"

Light police phone spark starter ten a dollar
All fire marcher explodes an invention
Gates are out a million
Try outstart capricious air
Mister tallhat revolver is everywhere

WHY WILL NOT LAMBS STAY FOREVER WELL IN SKINS?

It may be two men met Sunday ten with a happiness beast
A raw Lamb coming from the hollow
Tied to killer Bishops for the feast

100,000 Negroes most of whom have thin black skin
Tinderfoot passover dry edge light wells away
Blowup a million

TEMPER IS CANDY TO CAIN'S DAISY

In meetings red with Rosy pies
All were had by a good time up Ash's hollow

One narrow lane saved Lamb's friend Paschal Cain

III. HYMNS OF LOGRAIRE

1.
Nearer my God to rock of eyes
Or to my chariot of thee
That is Elias rider of red skies

Nearer my cherubim
To the crimson fruit
In chariot three

Wishing everybody well
From now to Monday.

2.
Sign on the dome:
"Expect thy next tread
Don't tread on the marine."

3.

You were sixteen
My village queen
Shining in sunpeel paint
With your strip all recent
From customary behaviour

You stood alarmed
O darkeyed think
Full to the very barrels
And I wished you cunning
Glasses and all

Which was the time
We broke the furniture
Trying to get me over
My own wall.

NORTH

PROLOGUE

WHY I HAVE A WET FOOTPRINT ON TOP OF MY MIND

To begin a walk
To make an air
Of knowing where to go
To print
Speechless pavements
With secrets in my
Forgotten feet
Or go as I feel
Understand some air
Alone
Around the formerly known
Places

Like going
When going is knowing
(Forgetting)

To have passed there
Walked without a word
To have felt
All my old grounds
Forgotten world
All along
Dream places
Words in my feet
Explain the air of all
Feel it under (me)
Stand
Stand in the unspoken
A cool street
An air of legs
An air of visions

Geography.
I am all (here)
There!

WEST

I. DAY SIX O'HARE TELEPHANE

Comes a big slow fish with tailfins erect in light smog
And one other leaves earth
Go trains of insect machines
Thirtynine generals signal eight
Contact barrier four

A United leaves earth
Square silver bug moves into shade under wing building

Standby train three black bugs indifferent
A week after he got sick
A long beetle called Shell
On a firm United basis
Long heavy-assed American dolphin touches earth
Please come to the counter
Where we have your camera
Eastern Airlines has your camera
And two others drink coffee
Out of yellow paper cups

Big Salvador not cooled off yet
From sky silver but
Hotel Fenway takes off at once
To become Charles' Wain

"The wise man who has acquired mental vacuity is not concerned
    with contemplation or its absence"
Forty stories of window seats available
Watcher stands on turntable ensemble
Counts passing generals
In curtains and spaces leaving earth
Two bugs like trucks
With airplane's noses
Ride our fables
Armored with earmuffs
Racing alone across asphalt sound
Armored against desert
All members
Not numbered yet

All clear neons come to the confession
The racing numbers
Are not remembered

Big Panam leaves earth
Gets Tax Man started into death
I'll get the teachers expanded
Turn your hat
Over your breath
Small dapper North Central is green for woods
And arrives safe
Flight information requires Queen
All green Braniff leaves earth for Pole
And big United Doppelganger slides very close
Seeking the armed savers

It points at us all and it is named:
"PHILIP."
It swings. Body No.7204 U
In case of mountain death
Discovers Teacher Jackson
Wins Colorado team maybe
In the snow
In the rare acts

Check tables for Vance Cooper
Advance with boarding arts
The glide area has now won and
Boy you got a lotta SPREAD

Hello say the mignonnes
You can go to bed
You can go to the gorgeous
Community period and

"Though appearing to act he does not engage in action."

Muffled the vice of Lou'ville smoke
The front

Hello money got to go pump earnings
Into bug MM2 for Derby Dad
Telling arrival is a copperhead
Big Mafia sits with mainlining blonde
Regular Bounder Marlo
Come meet world muffin at ticket counter
Ticket country
Mr. Kelsey
Mr. Kelsey
You are now wanted
In ticket country
"It is not distant and it is not the object of attainment."

Come we will pump our money into dogs
And lift our gorgeous raids sky high
Over the sunlit periods
Bending aluminum angels and Tax Man
And giddy grey girls
Over the suburban highschools
Our glide has won
Our teacher has dropped out
Our giant vocal captains are taking off
Whooping and plunging like world police
On distant outside funnels
Stainless diagrams sink
Into muddy air
We leave earth and act
Going to San
Patterns slide down we go for clear
Sanitation heaven
Combing the murky
Surface of profit
San Franciscan wing over abstract
Whorls wide sandpits watershapes
Forms and prints and grids

Invent a name for a town
Any town
"Sewage Town."
And day six is a climbing sun
A day of memory.

"Having finally recognized that the Self is Brahman and that
    existence and non-existence are imagined, what should such a
    one, free of desires, know, say or do?"
Should he look out of the windows
Seeking Self-Town?
Should the dance of Shivashapes
All over flooded prairies
Make hosts of (soon) Christ-Wheat
Self-bread which could also be
Squares of Buddha-Rice
Or Square Maize about those pyramids
Same green
Same brown, same square
Same is the Ziggurat of everywhere
I am one same burned Indian
Purple of my rivers is the same shed blood
All is flooded
All is my Vietnam charred
Charred by my co-stars
The flying generals.

"He who sees reality in the universe may try to negate it."

To deny linoleum badges
Deride the false tile field floor
Of the great Illinois bathroom
Lettered all over
With busy-signals

To view the many branches of the Shiva-cakes
The veined paddies or pastries
The burned trays of the Ming prairie
Or the porcelain edges
Of the giant Mother Mississippi

"His actions in this world are appearances only."

Appearances of a city
And disappearances
Dubuque dragging its handkerchiefs
Into a lake of cirrus
(Gap with one long leg of extended highway)
Compasses
Veiled
Valed
Vale!

"Not seeing, he appears to see."

A lake of cottons
Iowa needs names

High above this milk
There is a race-leader or power passenger
At odds with the white rest
The cloud captains
An individual safe
A strong-box enclosed self
A much more jealous reason
One among many
Who will have his way
A logical black provider
For only one family
Flying with a fortune in stamps

He stands in line with the others
Outside the highest toilet in the world
To establish a record in rights
High above the torment
Of milling wind and storms
We are All High Police Thors
Holding our own weapons
Into the milk mist each alone
As our battering ram
Fires us all into Franciscan West
As strangers in the same line
United in indifferent skies
Where nobody needs any anger.

    Not seeing he is thought to be over Sioux Falls
    Getting hungry
    Not seeing he is thought to see
    Saying "It is there"
    The family combination shelter and fun
    Room where all is possible.

Sinbad returning from the vines of wire
Makes his savage muffled voice
With playboy accents
To entertain the momentary mignonnes
As if he meant it all in fun

Sinbad returning from Arab voices
With his own best news for everybody boy
Says: "Wellfed cities
Are all below
Standing in line
Beneath enormous gas
Waiting to catch our baseball."

Sinbad the voyager makes his muscles of utterance
Soundless lips entertain the merveilles
Merveilles les vignes
De fil de fer
Hongrie
Les vagues barbares de l'est
Get ready for your invasion baby
Dr. Farges awaits you with his syringe
And Tom Swift rides by below
On his invisible mammoth mountains of art
The granite sides of Rushmore
Now showing four Walt Whitmans
Who once entrusted the nation to rafts

Four secret presidents
With stone ideas
Who mumble under gas
Our only government
Has provided free and says:
"This mildly toxic invention can harm none
But the enemy."

Merveilles! Secrets! Deadly plans for distant places!
And all high males are flying far west
In a unanimous supermarket of beliefs
Seeking one only motto
For "L'imagination heureuse":
WHY NOT TRY EVERYTHING?

III. GHOST DANCE: PROLOGUE

AMERICAN HORSE FAST THUNDER SPOTTED
HORSE PRETTY BACK GOOD LANCE PRESENT
NOV 27 1890

We were made many promises by the Commissioners but we never
heard from them since.
They talked nice to us and after we signed they took our land cut
down our rations.
They made us believe we would get full sacks if we signed but
instead our sacks are empty.
Our chickens were all stolen our cattle were killed our crops were
entirely lost because we were absent talking with the Commission.
We are told if we do as white men do we will be better off but we
are getting worse off every year.

When we were in Washington the President
The Secretary the Commissioner promised
We would get back a million lbs. of beef
Taken from us and the Bill
Passed Congress
But the Commissioner
Refused
To give us
Any meat.   *1969*

THE ORIGINATORS

Because I chose to hear a special thunder in my head
Or to see an occipital light my choice
Suddenly became another's fate
He lost all his wheels
Or found himself flying.

And when the other's nerve ends crowed and protested
In the tame furies of a business gospel
His feeling was my explosion
So I skidded off his stone head
Blind as a bullet
But found I was wearing his hat.

Thus in art and innocence we fix each other fates
We drink each other to gravestones.

Brothers and Sisters I warn you my ideas
Get scarlet fever every morning
At about four and influence goes out of my windows
Over the suburbs
Get out of the way of my ideas.

I am wired to the genius you donated, the general demon.

So one man's madness is another man's police
With everybody's freedom we are all in jail
O Brothers and Sisters here we go again
Flip-flopping all over the circus
With airs of invention.   *1977*

5: *To Belong to Allah*
To belong to Allah
Is to see in your own existence
And in all that pertains to it
Something that is neither yours
Nor from yourself,
Something you have on loan;
To see your being in His Being,
Your subsistence in His Subsistence,
Your strength in His Strength:
Thus you will recognize in yourself
His title to possession of you
As Lord,
And your own title as servant:
Which is Nothingness.

7: *To a Novice*
Avoid three kinds of Master:
Those who esteem only themselves,
For their self-esteem is blindness;
Those who esteem only innovations,
For their opinions are aimless,
Without meaning;
Those who esteem only what is established;
Their minds
Are little cells of ice.

All these three
Darken your inner light
With complicated arguments
And hatred of Sufism.

He who finds Allah
Can lack nothing.
He who loses Allah
Can possess nothing.

He who seeks Allah will be made clean in tribulation,
His heart will be more pure,
His conscience more sensitive in tribulation
Than in prayer and fasting.
Prayer and fasting may perhaps
Be nothing but self-love, self-gratification,
The expression of hidden sin
Ruining the value of these works.
But tribulation
Strikes at the root!   1977

THE MAN OF TAO

The man in whom Tao
Acts without impediment
Harms no other being
By his actions
Yet he does not know himself
To be "kind," to be "gentle."

The man in whom Tao
Acts without impediment
Does not bother with his own interests
And does not despise
Others who do.
He does not struggle to make money
And does not make a virtue of poverty.

He goes his way
Without relying on others
And does not pride himself
On walking alone.
While he does not follow the crowd
He won't complain of those who do.
Rank and reward
Make no appeal to him;
Disgrace and shame
Do not deter him.
He is not always looking
For right and wrong
Always deciding "Yes" or "No."
The ancients said, therefore:
"The man of Tao
Remains unknown
Perfect virtue
Produces nothing
'No-Self'
Is 'True-Self.'
And the greatest man
Is Nobody."   *1977*

The Turtle

Chuang Tzu with his bamboo pole
Was fishing in Pu river.

The Prince of Chu
Sent two vice-chancellors
With a formal document:
"We hereby appoint you
Prime Minister."

Chuang Tzu held his bamboo pole.
Still watching Pu river,
He said:
"I am told there is a sacred tortoise,
Offered and canonized
Three thousand years ago,
Venerated by the prince,
Wrapped in silk,
In a precious shrine
On an altar
In the Temple.

"What do you think:
Is it better to give up one's life
And leave a sacred shell
As an object of cult
In a cloud of incense
Three thousand years,
Or better to live
As a plain turtle
Dragging its tail in the mud?"

"For the turtle," said the Vice-Chancellor,
"Better to live
And drag its tail in the mud!"

"Go home!" said Chuang Tzu.
"Leave me here
To drag my tail in the mud!"   *1977*

WHERE IS TAO?

Master Tung Kwo asked Chuang:
"Show me where the Tao is found."
Chuang Tzu replied:
"There is nowhere it is not to be found."
The former insisted:
"Show me at least some definite place
Where Tao is found."
"It is in the ant," said Chuang.
"Is it in some lesser being?"
"It is in the weeds."
"Can you go further down the scale of things?"
"It is in this piece of tile."
"Further?"
"It is in this turd."
At this Tung Kwo had nothing more to say.
But Chuang continued: "None of your questions
Are to the point. They are like the questions
Of inspectors in the market,
Testing the weight of pigs
By prodding them in their thinnest parts.
Why look for Tao by going 'down the scale of being'
As if that which we call 'least'
Had less of Tao?
Tao is Great in all things,
Complete in all, Universal in all,
Whole in all. These three aspects
Are distinct, but the Reality is One.

"Therefore come with me
To the palace of Nowhere
Where all the many things are One:
There at last we might speak

Of what has no limitation and no end.
Come with me to the land of Non-Doing:
What shall we there say—that Tao
Is simplicity, stillness,
Indifference, purity,
Harmony and ease? All these names leave me indifferent
For their distinctions have disappeared.
My will is aimless there.
If it is nowhere, how should I be aware of it?
If it goes and returns, I know not
Where it has been resting. If it wanders
Here then there, I know not where it will end.
The mind remains undetermined in the great Void.
Here the highest knowledge
Is unbounded. That which gives things
Their thusness cannot be delimited by things.
So when we speak of 'limits,' we remain confined
To limited things.
The limit of the unlimited is called 'fullness.'
The limitlessness of the limited is called 'emptiness.'
Tao is the source of both. But it is itself
Neither fullness nor emptiness.
Tao produces both renewal and decay,
But is neither renewal or decay.
It causes being and non-being
But is neither being nor non-being.
Tao assembles and it destroys,
But it is neither the Totality nor the Void."   *1977*

SEVEN

ON BEING HUMAN

For My Brother: Reported Missing in Action, 1943

Sweet brother, if I do not sleep
My eyes are flowers for your tomb;
And if I cannot eat my bread,
My fasts shall live like willows where you died.
If in the heat I find no water for my thirst,
My thirst shall turn to springs for you, poor traveller.

Where, in what desolate and smokey country,
Lies your poor body, lost and dead?
And in what landscape of disaster
Has your unhappy spirit lost its road?

Come, in my labor find a resting place
And in my sorrows lay your head,
Or rather take my life and blood
And buy yourself a better bed—
Or take my breath and take my death
And buy yourself a better rest.

When all the men of war are shot
And flags have fallen into dust,
Your cross and mine shall tell men still
Christ died on each, for both of us.

For in the wreckage of your April Christ lies slain,
And Christ weeps in the ruins of my spring:
The money of Whose tears shall fall
Into your weak and friendless hand,
And buy you back to your own land:
The silence of Whose tears shall fall
Like bells upon your alien tomb.
Hear them and come: they call you home.   *1944*

FREEDOM AS EXPERIENCE

When, as the captive of Your own invincible consent,
You love the image of Your endless Love,
Three-Personed God, what intellect
Shall take the measure of that liberty?

Compared with Love, Your Triune Law,
All the inexorable stars are anarchists:
Yet they are bound by Love and Love is infinitely free.

Minds cannot understand, nor systems imitate
The scope of such simplicity.
All the desires and hungers that defy Your Law
Wither to fears, and perish in imprisonment:
And all the hopes that seem to founder in the shadows
    of a cross
Wake from a momentary sepulchre, and they are blinded
    by their freedom!

Because our natures poise and point towards You
Our loves revolve about You as the planets swing upon the sun
And all suns sing together in their gravitational worlds.

And so, some days in prayer Your Love,
Prisoning us in darkness from the values of Your universe,
Delivers us from measure and from time,
Melts all the barriers that stop our passage to eternity
And solves the hours our chains.

And then, as fires like jewels germinate
Deep in the stone heart of a Kaffir mountain,
So now our gravity, our new-created deep desire
Burns in our life's mine like an undiscovered diamond.

Locked in that strength we stay and stay
And cannot go away
For You have given us our liberty.

Imprisoned in the fortunes of Your adamant
We can no longer move, for we are free.   *1947*

WHETHER THERE IS ENJOYMENT IN BITTERNESS

This afternoon, let me
Be a sad person. Am I not
Permitted (like other men)
To be sick of myself?

Am I not allowed to be hollow,
Or fall in the hole
Or break my bones (within me)
In the trap set by my own
Lie to myself? O my friend,
I too must sin and sin.

I too must hurt other people and
(Since I am no exception)
I must be hated by them.

Do not forbid me, therefore,
To taste the same bitter poison,
And drink the gall that love
(Love most of all) so easily becomes.

Do not forbid me (once again) to be
Angry, bitter, disillusioned,
Wishing I could die.

While life and death
Are killing one another in my flesh,
Leave me in peace. I can enjoy,
Even as other men, this agony.

Only (whoever you may be)
Pray for my soul. Speak my name
To Him, for in my bitterness
I hardly speak to Him: and He
While He is busy killing me
Refuses to listen.   *1957*

THE FALL

There is no where in you a paradise that is no place and there
You do not enter except without a story.

To enter there is to become unnameable.

Whoever is there is homeless for he has no door and no identity
    with which to go out and to come in.

Whoever is nowhere is nobody, and therefore cannot exist except
    as unborn:
No disguise will avail him anything

Such a one is neither lost nor found.

But he who has an address is lost.

They fall, they fall into apartments and are securely established!

They find themselves in streets. They are licensed
To proceed from place to place
They now know their own names
They can name several friends and know
Their own telephones must some time ring.

If all telephones ring at once, if all names are shouted at once and
    all cars crash at one crossing:
If all cities explode and fly away in dust
Yet identities refuse to be lost. There is a name and number for
    everyone.

There is a definite place for bodies, there are pigeon holes for
    ashes:
Such security can business buy!

Who would dare to go nameless in so secure a universe?
Yet, to tell the truth, only the nameless are at home in it.

They bear with them in the center of nowhere the unborn flower
    of nothing:
This is the paradise tree. It must remain unseen until words end
    and arguments are silent.   *1977*

A CAROL

When Jesus got my broken back for Christmas, Juniors,
He learned what bloody parties seed from my sun

He'd try my tissues with the simple question
About the fire and water mixing in fun

(O bloody water
Never trust
The military sun)

The chance of ages is a rock you'll jump from, Juniors,
When Jesus has my waterwings and is alone out there
Out in the sea where I must swim my Spanish
Around the Puerto and the lucky phare

(O bloody noses
Never trust
The military air)

And so I come to learn a new religion, Princess Mabel,
O heavy Princess let me leap as I feel
Over the burning houses and the drowned dinner table
With my skinny Baptist and my Catherine Cart-Wheel
While Elders sell the pieces of my automobile

(O never waste
Good money on
An automobile)

So Juniors see my borrowed body in the stable
Cutting one more cold night out of the funeral's domain
O Master of Timetables who will be the lucky one?

When Jesus gets my broken back for Christmas
And so many wizard babies of God are chosen
To ride in a runaway train?

(O bloody water
Never trust
The military rain).   *1977*

ANTIPOEM I

O the gentle fool
He fell in love
With the electric light
Do you not know, fool,
That love is dynamite?

Keep to what is yours
Do not interfere
With the established law

See the dizzy victims of romance
Unhappy moths!
Please observe
This ill-wondered troth.

All the authorities
In silence anywhere
Swear you only love your mind
If you marry a hot wire.

Obstinate fool
What a future we face
If one and all
Follow your theology

You owe the human race
An abject apology.   *1977*

WITH THE WORLD IN MY BLOOD STREAM

I lie on my hospital bed
Water runs inside the walls
And the musical machinery
All around overhead
Plays upon my metal system
My invented back bone
Lends to the universal tone
A flat impersonal song
All the planes in my mind
Sing to my worried blood
To my jet streams
I swim in the world's genius
The spring's plasm
I wonder who the hell I am.

The world's machinery
Expands in the walls
Of the hot musical building
Made in maybe twenty-four
And my lost childhood remains
One of the city's living cells
Thanks to this city
I am still living
But whose life lies here
And whose invented music sings?

All the freights in the night
Swing my dark technical bed
All around overhead
And wake the questions in my blood
My jet streams fly far above
But my low gash is no good

Here below earth and bone
Bleeding in a numbered bed
Though all my veins run
With Christ and with the stars' plasm.

Ancestors and Indians
Zen Masters and Saints
Parade in the incredible hotel
And dark-eyed Negro mercy bends
And uncertain fibres of the will
Toward recovery and home.
What recovery and what Home?
I have no more sweet home
I doubt the bed here and the road there
And WKLO I most abhor
My head is rotten with the town's song.

Here below stars and light
And the Chicago plane
Slides up the rainy straits of night
While in my maze I walk and sweat
Wandering in the low bone system
Or searching the impossible ceiling
For the question and the meaning
Till the machine rolls in again
I grow hungry for invented air
And for the technical community of men
For my lost Zen breathing
For the unmarried fancy
And the wild gift I made in those days
For all the compromising answers
All the gambles and blue rhythms
Of individual despair.

So the world's logic runs
Up and down the doubting walls

While the frights and the planes
Swing my sleep out the window
All around, overhead
In doubt and technical heat
In oxygen and jet streams
In the world's enormous space
And in man's enormous want
Until the want itself is gone
Nameless bloodless and alone
The Cross comes and Eckhart's scandal
The Holy Supper and the precise wrong
And the accurate little spark
In emptiness in the jet stream
Only the spark can understand
All that burns flies upward
Where the rainy jets have gone
A sign of needs and possible homes
An invented back bone
A dull song of oxygen
A lost spark in Eckhart's Castle.
World's plasm and world's cell
I bleed myself awake and well

Only the spark is now true
Dancing in the empty room
All around overhead
While the frail body of Christ
Sweats in a technical bed
I am Christ's lost cell
His childhood and desert age
His descent into hell.
Love without need and without name
Bleeds in the empty problem
And the spark without identity
Circles the empty ceiling.   *1977*

Untitled Poem

All theology is a kind of birthday
Each one who is born
Comes into the world as a question
For which old answers
Are not sufficient.

Birth is question and revelation.
The ground of birth is paradise
Yet we are born a thousand miles
Away from our home.
Paradise weeps in us
And we wander further away.
This is the theology
Of our birthdays.

Obscure theology
On the steps of Cincinnati Station:
I am questioned by the cold December
Of 1941. One small snowflake
Melts on my eyelid like a guess
And is forgotten.
(Across the river my meaning has taken flesh
Is warm, cries for care
Across the river
Heaven is weeping.)

Heaven weeps without cause
Forever if I do not find
The question that seeks me
All the gates are shut
The monastery is cold
But everything here is certain:

Fire smoulders however
In the center.

Fort Thomas Kentucky
In a year of war
Is like Bethlehem, obscure
But not so innocent.
And I too am a prisoner
In a theology of will
While north of me a question
Is weeping in the snow
Because I am (for the time being)
A man without doubts
Renouncing the luxury of questions.

Wisdom grows like a flower
Turns her innocent face
In sweet compassion
South and west
Wondering about the seasons
Sun rain and nuns
Not knowing.

I am stubborn
I build ten theories out of stone
In a stone wall Eden
An unknown flower loves me more
I do not know it
The fire in the center
However is still there
And smoulders.

Heaven grows to a bird
With pretty wings
Her flight is like a question

Searching the south
For somebody.

Theology is sometimes sickness
A broken neck of questions
A helpless doubt
In an electric bed

The bird finds this doubt
Broken in the fever
And knows: "You are my glory
And I your answer—
If you have a question."

To sing is to begin a sentence
Like "I want to get well."
"I am not born for nothing
And neither are you:
Heaven never wept
Over nothing."

"And the ground of loneliness
Is love. The ground of doubt:
Is it truth?"

So all theology
Is a kind of birthday
A way home to where we are
Epiphany and Eden
Where two lost questions
Make one orbit
In the middle of nothing.
Is this the answer?

No one ever got born
All by himself: It takes more than one.
Every birthday
Has its own theology.   *1985*

I ALWAYS OBEY MY NURSE

I always obey my nurse
I always care
For wound and fracture
Because I am always broken
I obey my nurse

And God did not make death
He did not make pain
But the little blind fire
That leaps from one wound into another
Knitting the broken bones
And fixing sins so they can be forgotten

I will obey my nurse who keeps this fire
Deep in her wounded breast
For God did not make death

He did not make pain
Or the arrogant wound
That smells under the official bandage

Because I am always broken I obey my nurse
Who in her grey eyes and her mortal breast
Holds an immortal love the wise have fractured
Because we have both been broken we can tell
That God did not make death

I will obey the little spark
That flies from fracture to fracture
And the explosion
Where God did not make death
But only vision.

I will obey my nurse's broken heart
Where all fires come from
And the abyss of flame
Knitting pain to pain
And the abyss of light
Made of pardoned sin
For God did not make death

I always obey the spark that smacks like lightning
In the giant night
I obey without question
The outlaw reasons
The cries in the abyss
From this world's body that the wise have fractured

For God did not make death
He did not make prisons
Or stalking canonical ravens
The dirt in the incision

I will obey my nurse
I will always take care
Of my fractured religion

And God did not make death.   *1985*

LOUISVILLE AIRPORT

MAY 5, 1966

Here on the foolish grass
Where the rich in small jets
Land with their own hopes
And their own kind

We with the gentle liturgy
Of shy children have permitted God
To make again His first world
Here on the foolish grass
After the spring rain has dried
And all the loneliness

Is for a moment lost in this simple
Liturgy of children permitting God
To make again that love
Which is His alone

His alone and terribly obscure and rare
Love walks gently as a deer
To where we sit on this green grass
In the marvel of this day's going down
Celebrated only
By all the poets since the world began.

This is God's own love He makes in us
As all the foolish rich fly down
Onto this paradise of grass
Where the world first began
Where God began
To make His love in man and woman
For the first time

Here on the sky's shore
Where the eternal sun goes down
And all the millionaires in small jets
Land with their own hopes
And their own kind

We with the tender liturgy
And tears
Of the newborn
Celebrate the first creation
Of solemn love
Now for the first time forever
Made by God in these
Four wet eyes and cool lips
And worshipping hands
When one voiceless beginning
Of splendid fire
Rises out of the heart
And the evening becomes One Flame
Which all the prophets
Accurately foresaw
Would make things plain
And create the whole world
Over again

There is only this one love
Which is now our world
Our foolish grass
Celebrated by all the poets
Since the first beginning
Of any song.   *1985*

MAY SONG

It is May we are lost
In sunlight and leaves
Briars and moss

Your blue skirt
Is wet with melted ice
And Sauterne

The sun dries us
You tell me last night's movie
One I never saw. The woods
Are sweet with the sound
Of your voice
And all birds sing
That we are lost
In this part of the wood
Where no special scenery
Deceives the eye
And nothing can ever be
Consistent

Lost, lost the words of poems sound
And in your listening heart
Are finally found
In this heaven let me lie down
Under the fragrant tent
Of your black hair

Under those long lashes
I am again found
By your wise and lasting look
As all the hair of the sky

Comes slowly down
To bury me forever
In warm love
Here in the wood
Where we eternally come home
To taste the creation of life
At that soft point
Where the heart somersaults
And flutters against
Your bird heart beating wings
At the warm edge of lips

It is May we are lost
In unexpected light
We drown in each other
Can you still breathe
Darling in despair
I cling to the round hull
Of your hips and cry
Lend me for God's love
Your lifeboat
Your saving body
Save me body for I die
In the ideal sun
Cool me for I am destroyed
By too much perfection

It is May
We weep for love
In the imperfect wood
In the land of bodies
O lonely little boat
Carry me away
Across the sea of wine

O small strong boat
Bring me
My child.   *1985*

AUBADE ON A CLOUDY MORNING

Today no sun shines
Yet it is another morning
When in a distant room
Which I have never entered
No one sees your eyes first open
Only the dim light
Which is now perhaps at this moment changed
Into the light you look at
And the day that is known to you
Knows the moment of your return
From the rivers of night
From that nowhere
That ocean of sightless quiet
Inviolate unknowing where your heart
Slept for me
For me restored itself to life and to the love
By which alone I keep alive
For whose essential and direct messages
I am waiting now pacing up and down
In this uneasy lonely place
Waiting once again to live
And at war with my own heart
Because I cannot be there
To see your eyes reveal you
Opening not only to the light of my day
But to my own eyes and waiting heart

So that I might declare
As the one who knows best
That you are truly present again
That your identity
Has really been restored to the world
And your presence
The very necessary presence
And even the person of Love
Has been thank God granted us again
For another day in which I can
Again breathe, work a little,
Write something
(If I write for you
I can write something)
Try to exist
(If I am yours
I can exist)
Even though I am at war with my own heart
Because I am never by your side
When those eyes first open
To recognize the new day

But if this is at least a day
That is known to you
And now seen by your eyes
Though without a sun
Its dim light is enough
I am satisfied with it
I look for no other.   *1985*

Never Call a Babysitter in a Thunderstorm

Never call a babysitter in a thunderstorm you do not know
How the baby strong as God started all the thunder
In order to get attention
It is therefore useless to call on the phone

Never call a babysitter in the summer rain
When the baby has torn a hole in the ceiling
And the house is full of water all the lights are fused
You won't hear much on that phone

Tell her in vain to put the baby in the icebox
To keep him cool and dry
He will tear the icebox to pieces
And destroy the telephone

It is therefore useless to express your love
When the implacable baby strong as a tank
Plows through the walls of the house and blocks the highway
Yelling for shelter you can forget that phone

Never call a babysitter when the revolution
Is in full swing
Baby has hoisted the black flag and taken over
The telephone company and everything

When baby is holding off the police
With Molotov cocktails bazookas and hand grenades
You can forget about calling the babysitter
He has stuck a bottle of milk in her mouth
You'll never hear what she is saying

In short my boy be careful of love
It fills the world with this destruction

Millions of small pocket cyclones
Have fouled up communication with
Inexhaustible demanding rage

Rather than call her on the telephone
Which would only be an act of war
Go sell your car your golf clubs your tennis racket and your TV
Try to raise a little money
And pay the baby to set her free.   *1977*

CHEROKEE PARK

The elect are eating at long
Sunlit tables
Above our own trees
On airy Zion

But half way down
In the wooded hollow
We rock and swim
In love's wordless pain

No more doubts are left
To drown in
All is too plain and we hang
On the hillside above
The quiet woody gulf
Where one by one the cars
Float mutely down and sink
Without protest in the green tide
Of shadows

The wicked children
Of the elect
Pick up sticks
Whispering together
Run silently down
Into the gloom

To return slow
Climbing the hill in artful
Nodding silences with looks
And when they grow
To be business men they will know how
To beat love to death
Meanwhile

Half way between
Heaven and hell
Zion and the green river
We rock together
In that lovely desperate grip
Milled by the granite mountains
Of eternal consent
Deeper than the center of the earth
Before it is too late
Before you leave and go
To that other city where the cosmic fires
Are out and mills run smooth
For a profit

Under the maples we obey
The pure invisible machine
Hour by hour
Reduced to powdery
Perfect sand

This is the great impartial industry
The product of rocks
In dissolution and geologic time
For this we were destined
In love's other wars

The dry rapture of hopelessness
Purer than any joy
The clean desert sand
Of stark love without a puddle
Of consolation
The wrestling match
Of tender flesh with stone
The marriage of belief
With the unthinkable
Long time to the end
And the waking
Even higher in light
Than those elect tables
And in sunrise

Love on this silent
Hillside
Wars with need aim and time
And with humane summer
With both images of
Heaven and hell and high-low
Belief and the incredible
Yes and No

Contradicts everything
Flesh blood heart reason custom
Everything
And we do not care
In this unspeakable denial

Is our peace
We sit alone
Tossing cherry stones
On the bare places of the grass
In the green shadows.   *1985*

EVENING: LONG DISTANCE CALL

Tonight at dusk
Twenty warblers
None of which I could name
Glittered like jewels
On the power line
Now the moon is up
And they are gone

But a wood thrush
Still makes the cool shades twice lonely
For I am without you
And unable to forget it

You are two hundred miles away
With people I am not able to imagine
You might as well be gone
Into another country where love's language
Has never been spoken

Your voice in the night
Trembles with sorrow
But what can we do? True Love
Is sometimes a celebration
Of agony
We are torn apart

The half moon stands in the sky
We are separate in strange places
Home is strange
For the desolate
Never say we love
Only because love is sweet
What is sweet about this bitter
Division? It is death
It is the devil's kingdom
We are two half-people wandering
In two lost worlds

The half moon stands in the sky
We put down our phones
Love no longer
Even dimly sings in the long wires
To that impossible city

How desolate love seems
Now that even our sobs
Are silent.   *1985*

CANCER BLUES

It's a long hot night for cancer blues I sing
I listen to the tree frogs and rain while someplace
Else my Baby grows to be a magic Indian healer
My sweet Babe with special ways to fight a fever and cure
The biting black root-idea
With levelheaded advice and love for the hopeless hunted
SOUL.

It is a long night of rain to pass my time with cancer of the heart
But my Baby glows like medicine out there in the dark
Growing to be a living healer and radium
I grub these roots alone in the mud I thrash around
In my solitary swamp amid the hot frog blues. But all the time
She grows a little wiser and draws near
With that sweet healing temperament and compassion
Busy knocking out the Cannibal
TRIBES.

All alone out here in a mess of wild
Animals I kick my cancer bucket around
And every move I make I sink a little deeper but my Baby
Every minute knows another new way to get me out again
For she knows how to heal
She grows to be the punishment of dark sickness and sin
She is a sweet relentless punishing
INDIAN

Busy knocking out the pioneer gold-hunting tribes
She grows another day more perfect and wise
Cleaning this town of racetrack vampires and sham aristocrats
For her fiery gentle healing light is half a mile
WIDE.

I am alone this long side of the city roof-
Tops and go down to my cellar blues
O Honey love away my cancer
With your distant radio-electric loving glance and your caressing
    thought
For today they have hit me hard in the city
They have beat me with their official chain
They have hit the easy places of my head with the heel
    of a clerical shoe
And I am now flying dead over the Town sending you

The rush signals of emergency love and dread
As I speed homeward full of cancer by the neutral
Highways out of Town.

It is a long night out in the hot frog unintelligent country
Where you listen to my faint cries of cancer fading out
But hold on Baby and believe and be a healer
Be an Indian photo-electric
CURE
And if you don't know any winner bet on the kind that runs
And if you don't know any music listen to the one
Who writes these cancer blues for you in the
unlucky country Out by this STONE.
Honey bet on the kind that tries and leave the others
Make it fast into hell with all the windows open
Sights flying out and down the chemical lit up channels
Right through the front door of the Cannibal
COMMAND.

It is a long time to forget how low we grow
Another night older Baby and alone while I
Am kicking that bitter cancer bucket out of my heart
While you become a lucky Indian
STAR
And now while you draw closer you point silently down
You never miss you point right down to the
ROOT CURE
All the way down in the sweet summer earth to clean
The hunted heart of the hell-blues because you are grown
Into a healer. You kicked the fever
And you won me Honey for keeps you won me
In the summer finals
Complete with cancer of the heart.   *1985*

SIX NIGHT LETTERS

I
Every beautiful night
Is our invention
Slow-turning skies
The long dance of stars
The empty roads and fields
Moonlit concrete
Shining flat-eyed buildings
Voiceless streets

The sleep of the machine
Is our invention

With the owl in the wood
The last car on my road
Is heard far
From any city
I turn in my sleep
Seeking a message
From the dark heart
Of secure night
A message of love

Love sends no telegram
Calls on no ordinary phone
Sends no picture talks on no tape
Buys no present
No ring no jeweled emblem
Even of stars
Love wants nothing
That has a place
In a big city window
Nothing that has a price

You come to me like a cry
Born of my own abyss and wild
Gulf born of my mystery
Breaking out of the untranslated heart-song
Of my most secret planets

You come to me
Like my sweet soundless moon

It is midnight
You stand over my heart
Like an invisible sun

It is midnight
You have come
Bringing the truth I need
You stand over my hell
I wake with a cry and loud tears
My dark house is full of comets.

II
Every beautiful day
Is invention and evidence
Of that one morning
When the fields of May forever
Sing their slow hymn

This is the morning when God
Takes you out of my side
To be my companion
Glory and worship

O my divided rib
It is good to be willing

To be taken apart
To come together

Wine is good
Only when made
Of this day's sun
When we wake in each other

Sun will shine
From our two bodies
When we walk in paradise wood
Looking and inventing
One May one love

We bring glad life
To all white-waving fields
To our handsome earth
And we go worshipping together
All over the world's heaven

Why then has the whole world
Forgotten love?
We will shine without caring
It is good for us
To be unknown

Like the sun's pure
Untouched wine
We love without care
In spite of every dead heart
And sick intelligence

The slow hymn of May is everlasting
And every beautiful day
Is our invention.

III
Now we can
We can love because
We are free of the world
Nothing it says or does can stop us
We are free
Of its hold

Therefore the whole world
Pretending to ignore our madness
Secretly requires
The small chemistry of pain
Delight and peace
That is our discovery

Though it is too singular
To need a patent
It is the whole world's
Greatest need

If we fail or refuse
To lay bare
Our own essential anguish
If we do not by ourselves
Invent our own remedy
With no help from another
The newest love in the world
(That ancient and first love that was new
In the unheard of beginning)

The world will not begin again
Tomorrow
It will cease to exist.

IV

Though it is a cloudy night the whole gloom
Dances with luck
A thousand lights
A phosphorescent sea
My house and my heart founder
In deepsea darkness and love
An ocean of fireflies

How can I sleep exhausted
In the midst of fortune
Or dream of this day
Deeper than any dream

Your clear eyes in the taxi
Astonished me with their love
Their wide candor
Born of the race of winners
That need no game to play and no maneuver
We no longer fear the bite
Of love's accusing fire
For we have told everything
How can I sleep exhausted
In the midst of fortune

Now we know each other
We need never be afraid
Of telling too much
But only of not telling
Everything

We know love is a school where lovers go
To learn each other
Forming each other with inexhaustible care
Like patient mothers

Slowly building in long silences
And repeated consent
Over and over
Each other's innocent new body

How can I sleep exhausted
In the midst of knowledge

Your gentle love
Still follows me with patient lessons
Quieter than night
Envelops me and will not let me go
Though you lie alone
Now miles from where I am
And I have only the faint fragrance
Of your lips and long hair

How can I sleep exhausted
Torn out of my dear school
To lie alone thinking of one day's lesson
Love's new geography and form
Love's new map and clear highway
Where there is no other traffic
Where we both now know
We ride without a block
And without any rival.

V
Love is not itself
Until it knows it is frail
And can go wrong
It does not run
Like a well-oiled machine
Is nonpolitical
Nobody votes for love

Love wins
Because it is bad business
And loses everything
Love can never really begin
Until both lovers
Are bankrupt

Love runs best
When it seems to break down
When no amount of driving
Can rev it
No amount of gas
Can make it go
Love runs well
When it runs by itself
Without the help of man
Love goes best
When we seem to resist
And then it starts by miracle
And runs on air only
Until the end of the world.

VI
I pour a little gold rum
On two blocks of ice
And begin another letter
I wonder
If you will still smell
The scent of twisted lemon peel
On the thin paper

Writing to you
Is like writing to my heart
You are myself
The loneliness here

(This silence lemon and rum
Ice tropic of fireflies
Absence of music)
Envelops me
Like your own loneliness
Exploring my dark wood
And my lost house
To find itself.   *1985*

FOR M. IN OCTOBER

If you and I could meet up there
In that cool cloud
Like two sun
Beams or birds
Going straight to South America
Or distracted spirits
Flying together innocent
In midair

Or if we could be
Together like two barges in a string
Or tight wandering rafts
Heading downriver to St Louis or New Orleans

If we could come together like two parts
Of one love song
Two chords going hand in hand
A perfect arrangement
And be two parts of the same secret
(Oh if we could recover
And tell again
Our midsummer secret!)

If you and I could even start again as strangers
Here in this forsaken field
Where crickets rise up
Around my feet like spray
Out of a green ocean. . .
But I am alone,
Alone walking up and down
Leaning on the silly wind
And talking out loud like a madman

"If only you and I
Were possible"

Never mind:
Tonight the moon is full
And (you over buildings
I over trees)
We will watch it rise together.

1985

FOR M. ON A COLD GREY MORNING

A grey good morning and rain
And melting snow
Far from any help
Or love, I am warmer
At least wanting you.

Sorry in the grey
Weather without lights
Far from any other center
I nurse one inner lamp
Our common need
Which is our common presence.

It burns alone
And still
In the wet dark and for us,
Lighting a dry place in me
I do not know
Because it is myself
Love's inner cell
Where I am glad to be a prisoner
Since I am prisoner with you.

While you come back to life in distant rain
Looking perhaps at the dark river
With blurred eyes
Still full of dreams
And think of me in my hills,
You wake in me, darling,
We are nearer than we know
Love has another
Place of its own
Nearer to you than hill or city:
Nearer than your own mirror
You wake in another room
And the bed where you slept
Is a nest in my heart.   *1985*

EIGHT

MERTON AND OTHER LANGUAGES

LE SECRET

Puisque je suis
Imaginaire
La belle vie
M'est familière,

Et je m'en vais
Sur un nuage
Faire un serein
Petit voyage.

Car le secret
Que je sais lire
Si je disais
Vous ferait rire.

Mon coeur est nu
Que rien ne cache
Et rien ne garde
Qu'il ne lâche,

Rien il ne sait
Rien il ne songe
Il ne vous dira
Nul mensonge.

Et mes deux yeux
Sont mappemondes
Tout je vois
Et rien ne gronde.

J'étais en Chine
Tout à l'heure
Et j'y ai vu
De grand bonheur.

The Riddle

TRANSLATION OF "LE SECRET" BY BR. PAUL QUENON

I might be defined
The imaginative kind.
My life is charmed,
Untouched by harm.
Fast or slow
Off I go
To view the scene
On cloud serene.
What secret I've read
I've left unsaid;
It'd make you smile,
Or puzzle awhile.
My naked heart
Betrays no art,
With nothing concealed,
And nothing to steal,
Nothing to know
Nothing to dream;
I tell no lies.
In truth, my eyes
Are globes that see
All lands and seas:
I never complain
Be it China or Spain.
I've been around
And always found
Great happiness,
Tremendous bliss.

J'étais au centre
De la terre
Où il n'y a pas
De misère.

Si je visite
Les planètes
Et les étoiles
Plus secrètes,

Dans la nuit
La plus profonde
Je suis personne
Et tout le monde.

Si je m'en vais
Sans souvenir
Comment pourrai-je
Revenir?

Ne cherchez pas
A me revoir
Je serai là
Sans le savoir:

Sans figure
Et sans nom
Sans réputation
Ni renom,

Je suis un oiseau
Enchanté:
Amour que Dieu
A inventé.

1977

At earth's deep core
I've seen no sore.
And if I fly
To spheres on high,
Or visit afar
Some secret star
In depths of night
Though quite profound
—to put it right—
I would be found
To be
No one and everyone.
When I fly free
Of memory,
You should not yearn
For my return,
Or try to see
Where I might be.
I'm there, unknown;
In nothing shown.
Without a face,
Without a name,
Without renown
Or any fame.
I am a strange
Enchanted bird:
God formed me—Love,
By his own word.

2004

Je Crois en l'Amour

Je crois en l'Amour
Qui dort et vit, caché dans les semences,

Et lorsque je respire mon printemps
Dans la fraicheur des sommets liturgiques
En voyant tous les arbres et les blés verts,
L'émoi s'éveille au plus profond
De mon être mortel: et l'adoration
Sonne comme les cloches légendaires
Qui entonnent leurs chants sourds au sein de l'océan.

Et quand le soleil géant de mon été
A frappé l'or de toutes mes gerbes
Je fais fortune: c'est là mon chant, mon capital,
Ma louange de Notre Dame!

O frères, venez me rejoindre,
Buvez le vin de Melchisédec
Tandis que tous ces monts régénérés
Chantent la paix, vêtus des vignes d'Isaïe:
Car c'est ainsi que naissent les poëmes
Dans le creux de mon coeur d'homme
Et dans le sein de mon rocher fendu!

1949

I Believe in Love

TRANSLATION OF "JE CROIS EN L'AMOUR" BY BR. PAUL QUENON

I believe in love
Which slumbers and quickens
Hidden within the grain.

And when I inhale my springtime
In refreshing summits of the liturgy
And see all the trees and green wheat,
A tremor awakens in the very depth
Of my mortal being: and adoration
Sounds like legendary clocks
That intone their muffled chant
In the heart of the ocean.

And when the giant sun of my summer
Has thrashed the gold from off my sheaves
I've made a fortune: those are my chants, my coins,
My praises of Our Lady!

O brothers, come join me,
Drink the wine of Melchisedech
While all these rejuvenated hills
Clothed with the vines of Isaiah
Sing praise.

For thus are poems born
In my crucible, this heart of a man,
And in the core of my sundered stone.   *2004*

THREE EPIGRAMS

FROM THE SPANISH OF ERNESTO CARDENAL

i
Suddenly in the night the sirens
Sound their alarm, long, long alarm:
The siren's miserable howl
Of fire, or death's white ambulance
Coming and coming down the avenues
Along the buildings, it rises, rises, falls
Grows, grows, falls and is near
Growing and dying. Neither a fire nor death:
       The Dictator flashes by.

ii
Shots were heard last night
Out by the burial ground;
No one knows who killed, or was killed.
No one knows a thing,
Shots were heard last night.
That is all.

iii
We wake up with guns going off
And the dawn alive with planes—
It sounds like a revolution:
It is only the Tyrant's birthday.   *1963*

When the Shoe Fits

FROM THE CHINESE OF CHUANG TZU

Ch'ui the draftsman
Could draw more perfect circles freehand
Than with a compass.

His fingers brought forth
Spontaneous forms from nowhere. His mind
Was meanwhile free and without concern
With what he was doing.

No application was needed
His mind was perfectly simple
And knew no obstacle.

So, when the shoe fits
The foot is forgotten,
When the belt fits
The belly is forgotten,
When the heart is right
"For" and "against" are forgotten.

No drives, no compulsions,
No needs, no attractions:
Then your affairs
Are under control.
You are a free man.

Easy is right. Begin right
And you are easy.
Continue easy and you are right.
The right way to go easy
Is to forget the right way
And forget that the going is easy.

1977

The Birth of the Sun

From the Spanish of Pablo Antonio Cuadra

I have invented new worlds. I have dreamed
Nights built out of ineffable substances.
I have made burning stars, subtle lights
Next to half-closed eyes.

       Yet never
Can I recover that first day when our fathers
Emerged, with their tribes, from the humid jungle
And looked to the East. They listened to the roar
Of the jaguar, the song of birds; and they saw
Rise up a man with a burning face,
A youth with a resplendent face,
Whose looks, full of light, dried up the marshes,
A tall, burning youth whose face was aflame:
Whose face lit up the whole world!   *1963*

The Two Palm Trees

From the Spanish of Miguel Hernandez

Love rose up between us
Like the moon between the two palm trees
That never embraced

Private rustling of the two bodies
Flowing in waves, to a gentle song—
The hoarse voice was torn,
Tormented. The lips were stone.

The need to clasp: it stirred flesh
Lit up bones with flame
But arms wanting to reach
Died amid arms

Love, the moon, passed
Between us. Devoured
Our lonely bodies.
We are two specters seeking
Each other: Finding
Each other far.   *1968*

CHAGALL

FROM THE FRENCH OF RAISSA MARITAIN

Chagall came with long strides
Out of melancholy Russia
With a pack on his back
Full of violins and roses
With lovers lighter than angels
And frock-coated beggars
Musicians and archangels
And synagogues

He has meadows and villages
Rocking in the storm
Inns dances and beauties
Windows in the rainbows
Lily thrones for the brides
Under the silk scarlet canopy
The whole Bible in pictures
All the great personages

Longbearded and longrobed
With their lambs and pigeons
Spangled cocks and cows
Animals from the Ark and La Fontaine

Crowds and weddings kisses and tears
Chimerical horses
Ladies and cavaliers
Circuses
He has painted all the world
And nothing is left out
All the colors of the sun
Are dancing there

Then he has a Christ
Spread across a lost world
In a vast ivory space
At His feet a candlestick is lit
With six candles by mistake
While in the sky desolate men
Watch what goes on

At the four quarters of the horizon
Fire and flame
Poor Jews from everywhere go their way
No one asks them to stay
They have no place left on earth
Not a stone to rest on
Hence they must lodge at last in heaven
The wandering Jews
Whether alive or dead
With those friends of Chagall
Who here below have it so bad
They are always in the air on clouds
These pensive rabbis

And players of violins
Who make music
On their own hearts
In the snow   *1968*

BLACK STONE ON TOP OF A WHITE STONE

FROM THE SPANISH OF CÉSAR VALLEJO

I shall die in Paris, in a rainstorm,
On a day I already remember.
I shall die in Paris—it does not bother me—
Doubtless on a Thursday, like today, in autumn.

It shall be a Thursday, because today, Thursday
As I put down these lines, I have set my shoulders
To the evil. Never like today have I turned
And headed my whole journey to the ways where I am alone.

César Vallejo is dead. They struck him,
All of them, though he did nothing to them.
They hit him hard with a stick and hard also
With the end of a rope. Witnesses are: the Thursdays,
The shoulder bones, the loneliness, the rain and the roads. . . .

1963

BUTTERFLY

FROM THE SPANISH OF NICANOR PARRA

In the garden that seems an abyss
A butterfly catches the eye:
Interesting, the zigzag flight
The brilliant colors
And the black circles
At the points of the wings.
Interesting
The form of the abdomen.

When it turns in the air
Lit by a green ray
As when it gets over the effect
Produced by dew and pollen
Clinging to the obverse of a flower
I do not let it out of sight
And if it disappears
Beyond the railings of the garden fence
At an excessive speed
Or because the garden is small
I follow mentally
For a moment or two
Until I recover
My reason.   *1968*

Poetry Ends with Me

FROM THE SPANISH OF NICANOR PARRA

I do not claim to put an end to anything
I have no illusions in this matter
I would like to go on with my verses
But inspiration has come to an end.
Poetry has enjoyed good health
My health has been
Terribly bad.

What do I gain by saying
I have been in good health
Poetry has been sick
When all know that I am the guilty one.

So that's fine: I pass for a fool!

Poetry has been in the best of health
My health has been
Terribly bad.
Poetry ends with me.   *1968*

ONE / GEOGRAPHY'S LANDSCAPES (PP. 1–22)

AUBADE: LAKE ERIE

p.4. **Aubade**: borrowed from the French, meaning music to celebrate the dawn.

AUBADE—HARLEM

p.5. **Baroness C. de Hueck**: the Russian émigrée who had established a settlement house in Harlem for black Americans (Friendship House) where Merton volunteered in the summer of 1941.

FIGURES FOR AN APOCALYPSE

p.9–14 "In the Ruins of New York"; "Landscape: Beast"; "The Heavenly City": three sections from *Figures for an Apocalypse*, collected in 1947. "The Heavenly City" (p. 13) alludes to the New Jerusalem described in St. John's The Book of Revelation.

SONGS OF EXPERIENCE; INDIA, ONE

p.21. **Mother Oberoi**: Merton parodies the lavish Oberoi Hotel in Darjeeling, where he spent a night on his Asian journey in 1968.

TWO / POEMS FROM THE MONASTERY (PP. 23–48)

THE TRAPPIST ABBEY: MATINS

p.26. **Matins**: the name first given to Lauds, or prayers of the morning, said near the time of sunrise. There are seven such "offices" in the day of the Trappist monastic orders: Night Vigils, Lauds, Tierce, Sext, None, Vespers, and Compline.

AFTER THE NIGHT OFFICE—GETHSEMANI ABBEY

p.31. **Night Office**: prayers said at 2 or 3 a.m., when the monks begin their day; also known as Night Vigils.

p.32. **Mount Olivet**: the name which Merton gave to the hill near the Abbey where he later built his hermitage; allusion to the location of the Garden of Gethsemani and the Ascension of Christ in New Testament scriptures. **"Gideon's fleece"**: the wool laid out by Gideon, the ancient Hebrew military leader, in order to confirm God's direction to him (see Judges 6: 37–40).

THE READER

p.37. **Reader**: the monk designated to read from sacred and literary texts while the other monks take their meals in the refectory. The reader would stand in a small lectern lit by a single candle or light.

p.38. **pearls of water**: the drops of water left on the monks' fingertips when they dip them in the fountain of holy water on entering the refectory. The holy water signifies purification and blessing in the life of the monk.

ON A DAY IN AUGUST

p.39. **Saint Clare**: August 12th is the Feast of St. Clare (d. 1253), who followed St. Francis's teachings and devoted herself to the poor and sick.

A PRACTICAL PROGRAM FOR MONKS

This collection of aphorisms is a humorous satire on the monastic life.

p.48. **ne quid nimis**: moderation in all things ("nothing too much").

THREE / POEMS OF THE SACRED (PP. 49–73)

SONG

p.51. **Crossportion**: a neologism combining cross and portion, alluding to the monk's sharing in Christ's sufferings, and perhaps to St. John of the Cross.

SACRED HEART 2

p.51. **Sacred Heart**: the veneration of Jesus in which his fleshly heart is deemed the sacred metaphor of his love.

THE WINTER'S NIGHT

p.52. **Bridegroom's messenger:** allusion to the New Testament parable in which Jesus tells of the ten virgins, five of whom foolishly did not have oil in their lamps and thus missed the coming of the Bridegroom they were awaiting (Matt. 25:1).

THE BIOGRAPHY

p.55. *Consummatum est*: "It is finished"; an allusion to the last words of Christ on the cross (John 19:30).

ON THE ANNIVERSARY OF MY BAPTISM

p.59. **old St. Martin marked me for the cloister from high Canigou:** the church on Mt. Canigou above the town of Prades, France, where Merton was born.

SENESCENTE MUNDO

p.62. *Senescente mundo*: the end of the world.

p.63. **Jonas in the belly of our whale:** Merton adopts this as the archetype of his monastic life, in which he his hidden in the monastery by the will of God but against all expectation (Jonah 1:17).

EARLY MASS

p.63. **St. Joseph Infirmary—Louisville:** In 1950, Merton had surgery on his nose and was treated for colitis at this hospital in Louisville. It was the first time he had stayed away from the monastery since he entered in 1941.

HAGIA SOPHIA

p.65. **Hagia Sophia:** Holy Wisdom. This prose poem exploring the feminine wisdom of God is based upon the monastic offices: "Dawn (The Hour of Lauds)"; "Early Morning (The Hour of Prime)"; "High Morning (The Hour of Tierce)"; "Sunset (The Hour of Compline)"; and the Song of Songs, in which the coming of God's presence is in the form of the female figures of Eve (a healing nurse), a lover, the Virgin Mary; and Sophia, the feminine child. (See Proverbs 7–9).

p.65. *Natura naturans:* the laws of nature.

p.66. *Sapientia clamitat in plateis*: Wisdom cries out to all who will hear ("in the streets").

p.69. *Donum Dei*: gift of God.

p.69. *Exinanivit semetipsum*: annihilating Himself.

p.70. *tamquam a Domini Spiritu*: just as if the breath of God's Spirit.

p.70. *Salve Regina*: Farewell, Queen of Heaven.

p.70. *Ousia*: the fundamental principle of Being.

THE NIGHT OF DESTINY

This poem celebrates the end of the Moslem fast, Ramadan, and commemorates the giving of the Koran to Mohammed.

[UNTITLED]

p.73. **Amitabha**: the fourth Dhyani-buddha, personifying infinite light.

FOUR / SONGS OF CONTEMPLATION (PP. 75–102)

SONG FOR OUR LADY OF COBRE

p.78. **Our Lady of Cobre**: a shrine in the mountains of Cuba celebrating a miracle of the Virgin Mary, where Merton visited in 1940; he claimed that this was his "first real poem."

EVENING: ZERO WEATHER

p.81. **Assumption**: the Catholic doctrine that after her life on earth, the Virgin Mary was taken body and soul to heaven.

ELIAS—VARIATIONS ON A THEME

Merton created this long poem depicting the spiritual geography of the Hebrew prophet Elijah (I and II Kings) as resembling his own spiritual experience as a monk.

IN SILENCE

This poem strongly reflects the influence of G.M. Hopkins' poetics of "inscape" on Merton's writing. The stone walls of the monastery are "on fire," as is the world in Hopkins' "The World Is Charged with the Grandeur of God."

GRACE'S HOUSE

Merton's correspondent Elbert R. Sisson sent him a crayon drawing by his
daughter, Grace, included in a letter to Merton in 1961, which inspired
this charming and contemplative lyric. The drawing is archived in the
Rare Book Room at Columbia University.

O SWEET IRRATIONAL WORSHIP

p.96. **bobwhite:** quail.

NIGHT-FLOWERING CACTUS

p.98. The night-flowering cactus blooms rarely and nocturnally, provid-
ing the metaphor here for the coming of the Eucharistic presence of
God.

THE JOY OF FISHES

p.101. **Chuang Tzu:** a Taoist sage living sometime before 250 B.C.
Merton paraphrased his writings after reading a number of transla-
tions. He claimed *The Way of Chuang Tzu* (1965) as the favorite of
his books.

FIVE / HISTORY'S VOICES (PP. 103–41)

IN MEMORY OF THE SPANISH POET FEDERICO GARCÍA LORCA

Lorca (1898–1936) was killed at the beginning of the Spanish Civil
War. He is one of Spain's most revered poets and dramatists.

AN ELEGY FOR ERNEST HEMINGWAY

p.106. *ne cadas in obscurum*: unknown even in death; here, in obscurity.
p.107. *pro defuncto N{ominatim}*: prayer for a deceased man (from the
Roman missal).

MESSAGE TO BE INSCRIBED ON MARK VAN DOREN'S
HAMILTON MEDAL

Merton wrote this witty tribute to his mentor and friend Professor
Mark Van Doren, who received Columbia University's Hamilton
Medal for "the highest achievement in any field of human endeavor"
in 1959.

PAPER CRANES

The paper crane is the Japanese symbol for peace. In May 1964, a group of Japanese survivors of the atomic bomb visited Merton at Gethsemani; one of the women left a paper folded crane on his table. He wrote this poem in response.

p.119. **Hibakusha:** survivors of Hiroshima.

CHANT TO BE USED IN PROCESSIONS AROUND A SITE
WITH FURNACES

One of Merton's most acerbic and chilling writings, a trenchant and merciless satire on Adolf Eichmann's participation in the Holocaust.

A PICTURE OF LEE YING

Written after Merton saw a newspaper photograph of a young woman being deported back to China after fleeing to Hong Kong. Its caption was, "Point of No Return."

AND THE CHILDREN OF BIRMINGHAM

Based on accounts of black children facing police dogs, white mobs, and fire hoses in Birmingham, Alabama, during race riots in 1963.

PICTURE OF A BLACK CHILD WITH A WHITE DOLL

Merton wrote this elegy after seeing a photograph of what he called the "bomb-murder" of four black children in a church in Birmingham in September 1963.

SENECA

p.138. **Seneca:** Rome's leading intellectual and statesman in the mid-first century A.D.; he was a friend of Pontius Pilate.

ORIGEN

p.138. **Origen:** early Christian theologian (185–254), known for his writings on Neoplatonism and his sufferings for his religious devotion.

p.139. **Rufinus:** (345–410), translator of Eusebius' *Church History* into Latin, to which he added a book on Origen. ***beatus ignus amoris***: love impassions happiness. **Jerome:** fourth-century Church Father known for his translation of and commentaries on the Old Testament; an admirer of Origen. **Bede**: seventh-century English monk known for espousing the authority of Scripture over all other knowledge.

p.140. *Fornicationem efficassime fugiens*: most effectively avoiding fornication (i.e., through self-castration).

p.140. *Arturumque etiam sub terris bella moventem:* Even Arthur waging wars underground.

SIX / ENGAGING THE WORLD (PP. 143–78)

CABLES TO THE ACE

This long poem is comprised of eighty-eight cantos preceded by a Prologue in which Merton parodies his poet's voice and the macaronic language which he employs in this series of "cables" meant to satirize the debasement of language and the society which misused it. He claimed in a letter to James Laughlin that they could be read backwards or forwards with similar effect (*Thomas Merton and James Laughlin: Selected Letters,* 1997, pp. 321–22) and also that they are probably not translatable. Their sources are panoramic in scope and can be researched in Merton's working notebooks and reading library at the Thomas Merton Studies Center at Bellarmine University, Louisville, KY, which are supplemented by the available work of Merton scholarship.

#13 ("The Planet Over Eastern Parkway")

p.152. **Eastern Parkway**: the major boulevard leading to St. Joseph's Infirmary in Louisville where Merton went for treatment and where he met the student nurse, known by the initial M., to whom he formed a special attachment in 1966.

p.155. #75, #76: Merton refers to the "scandal" of his special friendship with M. as he envisions her in the corridor of St. Joseph's Infirmary where she works; he remembers the special Derby Day they spent together at the monastery when she visited him there in May 1966 (documented in his journals, published as *Learning to Love*, 1997).

p.155. #80: In this canto, one finds a possible glossary for interpreting the entire poem; here, Merton articulates his confidence that history unfolds into the compassionate redemption of Christ: "The disciple will awaken / When he knows history / But slowly / The Lord of History weeps into the fire."

THE GEOGRAPHY OF LOGRAIRE

Merton best explains this almost encyclopedic collection of antipoetry and macaronic language in his "Author's Note" before the "Prologue" and four major sections of this work. He writes: "In this wide-angle mosaic of poems and dreams I have without scruple mixed what is my own experience with what is almost everybody else's . . . . These poems incidentally are never explicitly theological or even metaphysical. The tactic is on the whole that of an urbane structuralism." Published posthumously (1968) and before Merton had finished this "work in progress," it was edited by James Laughlin and Barbara Harr at New Directions, who worked from his holograph notebook in which most of the poem had been composed. In *The Collected Poems of Thomas Merton* (pp. 595–609) there are extensive notes on the sources for this complex and subversive volume, based on Merton's study of the "Cargo Cults" and the influences on anthropology and history.

READINGS FROM IBN ABBAD

p.173. **Ibn Abbad**: Islamic theologian who became the leading mystical thinker in North Africa in the fourteenth century.

SEVEN / ON BEING HUMAN (PP. 179–219)

FOR MY BROTHER: REPORTED MISSING IN ACTION, 1943

This poem was composed in the days immediately following Merton's receipt of a telegram on Easter Monday of 1943 reporting his brother, John Paul, missing in action. His bomber aircraft had malfunctioned and crashed into the English Channel, where he died of a broken back and dehydration before the rest of the crew was rescued. He was buried at sea.